August 93

A souvenir of your vacation here in Switzerland.

"Än Guätä"!

Erika Berri

Culinary Excursions through Switzerland

Peter Widmer

Culinary
Excursions
through
Switzerland

SIGLOCH
EDITION

The illustration opposite the title page shows the preparation of a raclette at an Alplerfest. Raclette – a name which, as with roesti or fondue, unmistakably suggests culinary Switzerland. A festival in Valais is unimaginable without raclette, but in other regions of Switzerland and in neighbouring countries, too, the raclette triumphed long ago. Legend has it that raclette was invented in the vineyards of Siders in 1875 when the vintners lit a fire to warm themselves in the bitter cold. The mountain cheese they had brought along was too close to the fire and it melted. This melted cheese was unexpectedly tasty on bread, and a national dish was born. Today, electric raclette stoves are available which enable preparation of the dish in any household. Raclette prepared in the original manner over a wood fire, however, is still a special experience.

Recipe pictures photographed exclusively for this book by Hans Joachim Döbbelin.

Translation: Wolfgang W. Reichert

Switzerland, Yesterday and Today

The first traces of human existence within the boundaries of present-day Switzerland date back to the Old Stone Age, about 200,000 years ago. However, the findings are rather sparse and do not provide any conclusive evidence about the lives of these people. In the fourth century BC, nomads strayed in and settled down. Their knowledge of farming and animal husbandry paved the way for the development of the country. Providing food was no longer left to chance and coincidence, it became possible to keep a larder, and dishes and other ceramic household goods fostered permanent settlements. The invention of bronze- and iron-casting represented further milestones in the social development of man; settlements and villages appeared. In the third century BC, Celtic tribes, among them the Helvetians, made their way into the country and gave it a name still used today— Helvetia. However, the Romans, who were more powerful at that time, also subjugated the Helvetians, and the area of modern Switzerland came under Roman and, later, Ostrogothic, rule. During the Great Migration between the second and sixth centuries AD, the Alemanni settled extensive regions of Switzerland in its present boundaries. The West came under Burgundy rule and Graubünden under Ratian. Under the Merovingian Frankish kings and the Carolingians, all of Switzerland north of the Alps forms a part of the great Frankish empire after 534 AD. When it declined, Western Switzerland came under Burgundy, the rest to the Duchy of Swabia, and, therefore, to the German Empire. As time passed, the region was divided into many secular and ecclesiastic territories. The Counts of Savoy in the West, Kyburg in the East and Habsburg in the center were the most powerful noble families.

In 1231 King Henry, the son of Emperor Frederick II, presented the Urnens (inhabitants of Uri) with their freedom and promised never to ransom their land to princes. When the Schwyzers sent troops to Italy in 1240 to help Emperor Frederick II, he also bestowed upon them, as a "free people", their freedom. In the Spring of 1273 Count Rudolf von Habsburg bought sovereignty rights to Schwyz and Nidwalden, but they were not recognized by the inhabitants of the valleys. That was the beginning of the century-long antagonism between the Waldstatters and the House of Habsburg-Austria.

Switzerland as an independent political state is a country which has developed over seven hundred years of European history. In 1291 the three cantons Schwyz, Uri and Unterwalden united, in common defense against foreign forces, into an Everlasting League. The Ruetli oath "August 1, 1291: 30 men – perhaps there were more – have gathered on the village common at Ruetli, near a magnificent lake which is surrounded by giant, fog-shrouded peaks. They are tough and proud mountain farmers from Uri, Schwyz and Unterwalden, who have descended from their eagles nests, from their hillside farms which appear to be lost in the virtually inaccessible mountain reaches. They wear beards like prophets, have weathered faces, cut solid figures. These men are used to long marches, to difficulties, to working in the steep fields, to the daily struggle for life in sparse and wild surroundings which are unusually beautiful. They fear neither cold nor snow, neither rain nor the storms which shake the mountain peaks, strip the forests, strike down their herds and destroy their fields. Nonetheless, they are tired of having to daily endure the yoke imposed upon them by the Habsburgs, those Habsburgs who rule over a portion of Europe. Their feared satraps, the VOGTS, roam the land, collect tributes, and try to forcefully eliminate the old, traditional customs. A new order is to be created, an order which can be nothing but an unbearable form of serfdom. In signing the pact, the mountain farmers from Uri, Schwyz and Unterwalden swear before God and man to defend their freedom at any price." Professor Jean-Christian Spahni describes the events in his book "The Swiss Alps" although no one really knows exactly if it did happen that way and whether or not the legendary William Tell was present.

In any case, August 1 of the year 1291 is considered the hour of birth of the Swiss Confederation, written and sealed in the Letter of Confederation. After a long and difficult process of growing, and the pass-

Swiss farmers and Alpine cowherds love to preserve and follow their numerous popular customs. Alphorn players, yodeling groups, traditional folk costumes and the exchange of news and gossip are part of these.

ing of people, ideas, regions, time and events, in 1848 the old Confederation finally became the modern Federation of Switzerland.

The current national borders date back to the year 1815, when the cantons Valais, Neuchâtel and Geneva joined the Federation. The smallest political entity in this country is the community. There are over 3,000 communities, each of which governs local matters rather freely and independently: schools, taxes, roads, water, construction planning, and much more. The cantons developed from groups of communities which over the centuries grew together into tighter associations out of common interests or by the acquisition of the properties of former feudal lords.

Today, Switzerland has twentythree cantons (the canton Jura joined as the last in 1979), three of which are divided in two: Appenzell, Basel and Unterwalden. Each of these twentysix states within a state, Uri, Schwyz, Obwalden, Nidwalden, Lucerne, Zurich, Glarus, Zug, Bern, Fribourg, Solothurn, Basel-City, Basel-Land, Schaffhausen, Appenzell-Ausser-Rhoden, Appenzell-Inner-Rhoden, St. Gallen, Graubünden, Aargau, Thurgau, Ticino, Vaud, Valais, Neuchâtel, Geneva, Jura (listed in the order of entry into the Federation) has its own constitution, its own laws, its own parliament, its own courts and its own government. The Federal Government, or the Confederation, has been granted only some limited political powers by the cantons. These are specified in the Federal Constitution: foreign policy, national defense, the guidelines of economic policy including finances, civil and criminal legislation and others.

Sovereign in Switzerland is the citizenry of all Swiss men and women over the age of twenty. The confederate parliament consists of the National Council, elected directly by the people, and the Council of States, in which each canton has two members and one for each half-canton. Together, the chambers form the Federal Assembly, the legislative body of Switzerland. The executive consists of a Federal Council which has seven members, a Collegial Board which makes its decisions collectively, although each member administers a portfolio which corresponds to a ministry. Such a national government is indeed not particularly flexible, but does guarantee continuity and stability.

Switzerland is a multi-faceted country. It is polymorphic in its structure; the geologic, geographic, political and economic conditions cover a wide spectrum.

Geologically, Switzerland is divided into three natural geologic formations: the Jura Mountains, the Central Plateau and the Alps. Near Geneva the Jurassic Mountains branch off from the Alps and stretch in a north-easterly direction towards the Rhine. The Jura extends beyond the national borders into Swabia and France. The Central Plateau stretches in a general south-westerly direction from Lake Constance towards Lake Geneva. It is crossed by many ranges of hills and mountains consisting of the characteristic rock formations of the Central Plateau, of Nagelfluh, sandstone and clay. The deposits of the glaciers of the Ice Age (moraines) provide portions of the very fertile topsoil. The Swiss Alps comprise the middle and highest parts of the Alpine arch which stretches from the Ligurian Sea to the Danube near Vienna. They are, like the Jura, a folded mountain range. Their stratifications of limestone, sandstone, shale, granite and gneiss are not only folded but also pushed on top of each other in layers. In this respect, Switzerland presents itself as a geologist's dream.

These topographical and geographical characteristics contributed to the development of four linguistic and cultural regions. What differences there exist between Western Switzerland and the Appenzell region! How different it is in Valais compared to the area around Lake Constance, how great the differences in landscape between the Emmental and Ticino! Where the landscape, architecture and climatic conditions are so different, there are also differences in customs and language to be found.

The various Swiss-German dialects developed in the regions settled by the Alemanni, and French in the area of the former Burgundians, in Western Switzerland. The people in Southern Switzerland speak Italian, and about 44,000 Swiss in canton Graubünden keep to the old, lovely linguistic tradition of Romansh.

The differences in landscape, from the flatlands with the many lakes up to the regions of eternal snow, the variegated influences from all directions contribute to certain, distinct intellectual climates and typical characteristics. We only have to take part in some of the many festivals which take place throughout the year all over the country. Then we will better understand these characteristics and differences. Food and drink always play an impor-tant rôle in local traditions and in the activities of the population in all regions of the country and in all seasons of the year. We'll revert to this aspect within the framework of our topic again.

The old engraving shows the monastery on top of Mount St. Gotthard. The monastery used to be an important support basis and rest station for travellers on their dangerous journey across the Pass.

A War-like People

Generally, the Swiss are considered to be the epitomy of peace and stability. And in fact the Swiss did hang up the craft of war many centuries ago. There is probably no other people on this unreasonable planet Earth who have lived so long without conflicts with their neighbours, some of whom, even up to most recent history, have proved themselves to be much less peaceful. But they respect the peace-loving Confederation and its neutrality which has by now become proverbial.

But this was not always the case. In the late Middle Ages, the Swiss were hotly coveted by nearly every army in Europe as warriors because of their also proverbial wild boldness. They were even greatly feared, and their reputation was not always the best. They passed through the countryside as pugnacious, drunken, pyromaniacal, abusive, murdering hordes – drawn by adventure, corrupted by money. It is often said that the population explosion of the 14th and 15th centuries made it more and more difficult for the young Confederation to feed its people. Many are said to have been forced, therefore, to find their livelihood in the service of others. Even if times were hard then and the standards of living relatively low, a healthy country with healthy inhabitants should surely have found it possible to feed its children. Seen in this light, it is remarkable that the Swiss warriors were primarily recruited from the herdsmen of the Forest Country, since it was the Alpine farms with their booming dairy production that were relatively well off. The "poor herdsman of the mountains" had become rare. The daily, unfettered occupation with animals and cheesemaking, his basic work which determined the rhythm of and gave meaning to his life, enriched him and made him independent; this was the environment of the herdsman in those days. It was also the soil from which the type of herdsman grew and who, as a warrior and ruffian, unwittingly helped shape the history of the Confederation. These fellows who left wives and children, animals and flocks, to venture out into the world were called "army chasers", mercenaries who went out to seek their fortunes as soldiers in the service of others.

This style of herdsman soldiering, fundamentally

This copperplate engraving by Meister PW from the year 1499 is called "The Swiss War." According to the legend, Tell's shot at the apple triggered the rebellion of the Swiss against the Habsburgs. Meister PW vividly portrays how the Confederates – here around Lake Constance and the upper Rhine – fought for their freedom and privileges against Maximilian I and the Swabian League. In 1499 their independence was confirmed in the Peace of Basel. The text on the copperplate reads: "This is the war between the Roman King and the Swiss and the whole countryside; cities, castles and villages in Switzerland and a part of Swabia. And where an S is drawn, the Swiss are in power, the rest, the (Holy Roman) Empire. And the source of the Rhine and Danube, both."

·SVPPOSITA·PICTVRA·REGIE·MAIESTATIS·HELVETIORVB·CÕFLICTV·HIS IVVAT·
QVO·QVISB·LOCO·VICTORIA·POCIT?SIT·QVO·B·TERGA·PREBVERIT·HOSTI·OCVLARI·
DEMÕSTRACIÕE·EDOCES·IN·QVA·QVICB·HELVECIORVM·LOCO·S·LBA·PROPITVR·

·DIS·IST·DER KRICH·TZWICHSSE·DEM RVMICH SSE·RVNICK·VND·DEN·SWEITZERN·
VND·GANSE·LANTSCHAFT·STET·SLOS·VND·DVRFE·IM SWEITZ LAND·VND·EIN·
DEIL·FON·SWAB·LANT·VND·WAIR·EIN·S·STATT GETBEICHNITT·DAS IST DEN SWEITZ'
VND WORFE·DAS AND·DERICH·VND·DE·SPRVNCK VOM KEII VND·THOMAW BEIDE

different from that of the farmer or town-dwellers, was based often on a war-like spirit and drive for independence, basic human drives. They were grown and practiced in boys' groups and men's clubs, in forbidden self-defence meetings and private challenges, nurtured from early childhood by competitions and feats of arms, livestock rustling and hunting. This rough, natural, individualistic militia met regularly in armed conflicts as "blood brothers" or "free brothers". As a loosely-knit group of young fellows with a "lost cause" and a self-elected captain, these warrior groups, which were as ill-bred, youthfully anarchial as imaginable, committed those heroic deeds which "brought praise and honor to their fatherland." Things, which the careful, circumspect war council did not dare do in critical moments were accomplished by the self-sacrificing, self-assured and bold "free brothers" in their hour of greatness. Before and after the battle, however, this same wildness, misdirected, found its expression in murder and plunder. In raids in which the uncontrolled young Alpine natives grabbed, besides prayer books, diapers and headgear, the one thing they had plently of at home – cheese.

"For the Swiss, war was slowly becoming a way of life. The terrible halberd fighters feared no one. They proved this at Grandson where in 1476 they overran the army of Charles the Bold, which had been considered invincible. That was a hard blow to the Burgundian, from which he never recovered. The bounty consisted of immeasurable wealth. Gold, silver, diamonds and other precious stones filled their pockets, fanned greed and the lowest of passions. The peasants from Uri, Schwyz and Unterwalden consciously turned their backs on the mountains and dedicated themselves from then on to militarism. They made up a powerful military force which was available to serve princes and kings. Conscience became subordinated to materialism.

"The soldiers made lots of money and spent it without having counted it. They burdened themselves with neither scruples nor prejudices. They were not interested in art, science or culture. They became intoxicated with the adventures which they found on the road or battlefield. This was in fact a regression into the barbaric age of Helvetia.

"Soldiering meant unending blood-letting of people and energy. It depleted the defence forces of the country since the best and bravest men were lured out of the country with the bait of money and were estranged from their real chores." (Jean-Christian Spahni)

And while the Swiss warrior was risking his life in Italy, Spain or France, his trade in the mountains, which "brought the country gold, silver and great wealth", fell to ruin. Herds and cheese production declined. Once again, the women took responsibility for milking and cheese making. The thoroughly war-like life-style of the Alpine peasant herdsmen and warriors is expressed in the opinion of a foreign observer who said, "Cattlemen and herdsmen, who spend the day pressing and thickening milk, who live, so to say, without any laws and who are ignorant of God and the world, want to foist laws upon almost everyone else."

It took a long time before the mercenaries became reasonable again. "A new era was to begin for the country. Suddenly, the people remembered their mountains, which they had turned their backs on for centuries. They finally realized that their future was more likely to be found serving the fatherland than serving military adventures under foreigners, adventures which sooner or later would be doomed. This return to basic values is nature's revenge. The Swiss went from one extreme to another, ignored the outside world and suddenly experienced a deep love for those places which were and still remain the actual birthplaces of their culture. The mountains became the focal point of all activities. They were celebrated, glorified and praised in song." (Jean-Christian Spahni)

Many of the poor Swiss mountain farmers were enticed into the life of mercenaries in the service of foreign feudal lords. As widely feared warriors they were welcomed by many warlords who paid them well.

Two kinds of "swinging", but what a difference! If the Flag Swinging (Fahnenschwingen) (lower right) is widely known, the foreigner usually does not know what to think of wrestling in the so-called "swing-pants". This Swiss national sport was officially mentioned in 1235 and has remained popular up until the present. Thousands of spectators stream to the numerous "Swing Festivals" which take place all over the country in the warmer seasons.

From the Alpine Meadow Cooperative to the Confederation

As we all know, the old warped and idolized picture of a typical Swiss is still prevalent in minds and tabloids abroad. Of course, a Swiss can yodel, swing flags, milk cows and alternate between cheese- and watch-making in his chalet. We smile at this notion but fall into the same trap when we similarly picture the Confederates of 1291 as coming from the "people of herdsmen". This onesided view is wrong. Although the Germans and Helvetians already were dairy farmers at the time of the Romans, to a limited degree livestock raising and dairy production were not very important in our country before the beginning of the Confederation. Small amounts of cheese, usually made by women from sheep's and goat's milk, were only a supplement to the primary food of the time, namely grains, from oatmeal to rye bread. Nevertheless, cheese played a successful and important rôle in the economic development of the waning Middle Ages and the rise of Modern Times.

The basic unit of the early economic life were the communities. Wild water and avalanches could not be stopped alone, ditches and communal forests could not be built by one person himself. The milk one herdsman got in one day was enough for butter and soft cheese, but if he wanted to produce larger, exportable cheese loaves, he was dependent on the Alpine collective.

The Alpine collectives, real cooperatives and predecessors to our modern cooperatives, represented a compromise between common and private ownership. The individual's share in the common

"This country is framed by snow-white mountains, filled with golden meadows and silver lakes," shouted an American when he visited Switzerland for the first time. It is easy to understand him, this tourist from the New World, in light of this dream-like setting seen from the Rochers-de-Naye, looking out over Lake Geneva.

The Swiss know, of course, what chesse on the one and tourism on the other hand mean for their country. What could have been more natural than to combine them into an Alpler Festival, as is done annually in September in the Justis Valley high above Lake Thun. The cheese produced during the course of the summer by the herdsmen is brought to three log cabins – often with special carrying frames on their backs – where the cheese is stored. On one day in September, the Chaesteilet (cheese aportioning) draws numerous visitors to the Justis Valley. According to a precise, fixed procedure, the master herdsman distributes the cheese to the owners of the cows. Then the day ends with a festive feast.

meadows was not determined by area but by "cow rights," "batches" or "cow eatings". Whoever had summer rights for one cow or more was required to proportionally take part in maintaining the meadow. The founding and organization of the meadow cooperatives hardly ever went without severe collisions and incidents. Often the spiritual and secular interest payments had to be settled in tough negotiations or under threat of violence.

"Meadow and sieve books", necessary pillars of traditional customs, kept records of rights and duties. The oldest of such an "Alp-Book" is said to date back to 1423. Further developments need only be hinted at here: The new cheese-making technology at the end of the 16th century, especially the production of a Sbrinz or spale cheese, required a minimum of about thirty cows, and an especially industrious cow-herd, a professional cheese-maker, as it were, since the export trade was becoming more and more important. The art of cheese making and a good market could not, however, compensate for the disadvantages of collective ownership. Private meadows with enough animals, as well as the "capitalistic meadows" or "stock holding meadows" which were leased to herdsmen for a meadow fee, too, could be operated more economically.

The confederations of the Alpine valley companies into market, Allmend or meadow collectives are ancient, some are older than the Confederation itself. The most distinguished earliest and toughest of these still exists today under the name "Superior General Corporation of the District Schwyz". Such collectives, really private organizations, existed at the beginning of our nation. Their principle: a collective for the common good; rights and duties for all, democratically administered, served as godfather for our political order.

According to legend, the original cantons of Uri, Schwyz and Unterwalden were supposed to have been united into an eternal allegiance through the Rütli oath in 1291.
That year is recognized as the birth date of the Swiss Confederation.

From Emmental to Gruyère

Swiss cheese is – as everybody knows – world famous. It is not only the climatic conditions which allow the milk from healthy cows to mature into a first-class quality product in the fresh, crisp mountain air, but it is also a centuries-old tradition of cheese making which is carefully and meticulously cultivated and honored in Switzerland.

Even the ancient Romans knew how to appreciate the cheese of the Helvetians, and they brought home considerable quantities across the Alpine passes. The cheese produced by the Helvetians then was probably a kind of Emmental cheese, which means that this cheese can proudly look back on a two-thousand-year-old tradition. But in those days, cheese was one of the rare items on the menu, because even in mountain regions such as, for instance, in the Melch Valley or in the upper Schaechen Valley, more than half the fertile soil was cultivated. Peasants from Obwald brought surplus grain to market in Lucerne, Schwyzers took theirs sometimes across the lake to Zug. Under such intensive grain cultivation, there was little room to grow winter feed for large stocks of animals.

The successful defensive battle of the Swiss at Morgarten in 1315, and especially the brilliant victory over the Austrian Knights at Sempach in 1386, brought, in addition to the political decisions, important support for the Alpine meadow economy. Large granaries in the central plateau were now secure, the exhausting field work in the high valleys could be abandoned. Instead, the grassy areas supplied the necessary winter hay for the livestock of the mountain meadows. The economic focal point shifted from the valley floor to the high meadow, to the newly organized Alpine pastures. The grain farmer became a cow-herd. Milking and cheese making, previously women's work, became a man's job. From then on, the Confederation was divided into two economic groups: farmers and herdsmen. The herding country included primarily the Forest Country, the Entlebuch, the upper Emmental, the Berner Oberland and the country of Gruyère. The most famous Swiss cheeses are still made here to this day.

Switzerland had and still has some of the best pasture land and the healthiest livestock in Europe. With its central location which favors transportation, cheese production experienced a tremendous increase, which, beginning in the 17th century, laid one of the cornerstones for the wealth of the country. The demand for Swiss cheese was so great that the Alpine herdsmen could no longer meet it. Increased production meant larger herds and required new pastures. The high meadows were no longer sufficient, so cheese production was forced to move slowly lower down into the valleys. In 1815 the first village cheese work shop was founded in Kiesen between Bern and Thun. Today it houses a small museum in which the old equipment can still be seen.

As things go in the business world – the brilliant business success which Switzerland was having with its cheese did not go unnoticed by other countries. Soon there were numerous imitations. Even if the Confederates still maintain with pride, and probably justifiably so, that their cheese cannot be imitated, the monopoly was nevertheless broken. Today, "Emmentaler" is made in Germany, France, Austria, Finland – even in Argentina, Australia and the United States. Cheese, along with watches a synonym for Swiss export products, makes up only about one percent of all Swiss exports today.

So the Swiss place even more emphasis on the quality standards of their cheese. All original Swiss cheese loaves are stamped with the trade-mark "Switzerland" in wheel-shaped spokes. An ordinance issued only a short time ago by the former head of the Department of Commerce, National Council member Hans Hurlimann is intended to more sharply define and protect Swiss cheese. It is now clearly stated how long a cheese must ripen, how large and how heavy a loaf can be, the shape and size of the holes, and what color the cheese dough must have. Anybody who is interested can now obtain official detailed information from fat content to consistency.

Appenzeller cheese, for example, may have only tiny little holes "between three and four millimetres in diameter" and these are to be „rather sparingly and evenly distributed" in the loaf, which is to weigh

Cheese is one of Switzerlands most important export items. Its production dates back to a long tradition which, today, is still carefully cultivated. But pictures like these, nevertheless, will probably very soon be part of the past, forever. We see one of the few herdsmen who still produce mountain cheese completely in the old-fashioned way. The photos were taken at the Schwaegalp in Canton Appenzell and show herdsman Jakob Schiess from Hundwill at various stages of cheesemaking.

It's easy to imagine that such a mountain cheese tastes especially delicious and we are happy to see the industrious herdsman enjoy his pipe after a hard days work.

between six and eight kilograms. "The cheese is to be sliceable, between ivory and light yellow in color and the taste aromatic." Sbrinz from the mountain cantons and the central plateau has „no or only sporadic holes of 0.5 millimetre in size". "Sbrinz can be grated, planed and sliced." The herb cheese from Glarus, the "Schabziger" is "aromatic, strikingly piquant." Active and clever advertising does a little more to maintain the brilliant reputation of Swiss cheese.

Let's talk a little more about the three most famous Swiss cheeses, Sbrinz, Gruyère and Emmentaler in detail:

For a long time, scholars could not agree about where **Sbrinz** got its name. Latest research shows that the Sbrinz probably dates back to the same origins as the Romanian word *Brinza,* the designation of a kind of sheep's cheese, which was called *Brenza* in 1397 in Ragusa, but is called *Sbrinzo* in Italian. Now, when our cheese was taken through the Alpine passes to Italy from the Hasli Valley and became a favorite object of exchange for spices, chestnuts and wine there – about four hundred years ago – it was given the name Sbrinz without further ado.

Sbrinz is produced in central Switzerland, primarily in the canton Lucerne, but also in the cantons Unterwalden, Schwyz and Zug, from whole cow's milk. It usually contains 46 to 52 percent fat in dry state. The loaves, weighing between 20 and 40 kilograms which may have only occasional holes the size of a pin-head, are stored and cared for on special racks during the ripening process of two to three years.

Sbrinz is a hard cheese with full fat content and contains, just as does milk-fat, the fat-soluble vitamins A, D, E and K and the provitamin A, carotine, which gives the cheese its natural yellow color. Especially important are the protein components which are so abundant in Sbrinz. In addition, during the long ripening process, the casein content is extensively reduced so that it is easily digestible even by people with sensitive stomachs. Many of the dishes in the recipe section of this book call for this hard cheese.

Gruyère, which is called **Greyerzer** in German, is one of the oldest known of all hard cheeses. It is at home in the country of Gruyère, the fertile region on the edge of the Fribourg Alps. The earliest mention of cheese production in the Gruyère region is in a document by Count Guillaume, the first Count of Gruyère. This dates from 1115 and deals with the delivery of products from the Gruyère Alps to the monastery of Rougemont. The document mentions that the monastery is required to maintain the herdsmen's cabins and the necessary cheese tubs, sieves and cheese moulds, among other things. The earliest designation of this cheese as "Gruyère" from this region is documented in 1602. At that time the government of Fribourg offered the delegates of the French Embassy fourteen Gruyère cheese loaves as a gift.

Emmentaler is famous all over the world and is known outside Switzerland often simply as Swiss cheese. In order to produce an Emmentaler cheese of between 80 and 85 kilograms (175 and 190 lbs), the cheese maker needs about 1.000 litres (263 gallons) of milk. This corresponds to the average daily production of 80 cows. Thus for one kilogram (2.2 lbs) of this hard cheese we need about twelve litres (quarts) of milk.

How is Emmentaler cheese made? In a large cheese tub which is equipped with stirring equipment, the fresh milk is evenly heated for about 20 minutes until it reaches 32 to 33 degrees centigrade.

At this time, the cheese maker adds rennet dissolved in water, and bacteria cultures. Rennet is a fermenting agent which is obtained from the stomach lining of young calves. Within thirty minutes, the milk coagulates into a mass which is similar to yoghurt. Using a cheese harp, a stirring instrument which is strung with wire, the cheese maker cuts the mass for three quarters of an hour in a precise, fixed rhythm into pieces as even in size as possible, the so-called "cheese seeds". During this process, the watery part, the whey, separates from the cheese. Whey and cheese are then heated without stirring for thirty minutes to 53 degrees centigrade and are again stirred for three quarters of an hour by the stirring equipment. About two and one half hours after the addition of the rennet, the cheese is lifted out of the tub with a coarsely-woven hemp cloth to drain and brought under the press in a round wooden case 18 cm in height called a Jaerb. Now the cheese has been formed. It will be turned several times during the course of the day and compressed with continually increasing pressure.

The next morning it is taken into the salt cellar where it is first sprinkled with salt. After about twenty hours, when the young cheese loaf has completely cooled, it is placed in a highly concentrated saline solution and then stored on round wooden lids in the cool salt cellar for ten days.

In the warm, moist fermentation cellar, the fermentation of certain components of the milk creates carbon dioxyde, which partially collects in the cheese. This cause the famous holes in Emmentaler cheese, which inspired Kurt Tucholsky to pose the question, "Where do the holes in the cheese come from?" Tucholsky found no explanation which satisfied him – at least in a literary sense – so he decided, short and sweet, "A hole is where there is nothing."

Now, we know better, of course. The more evenly the process runs, which takes eight to twelve weeks, the nicer and more even the holes will be. Emmentaler is ready to eat in about four months, but it is still mild at this time. For a medium cheese we have to wait five to six months. Well ripened cheeses are even older.

We can't go into all Swiss cheeses here in detail. Some of them, such as the Schabziger from Glarus, the Appenzeller or the Raclette from Valais, will appear again in the recipe section. If you would like to get to know Tête de Moine, Tomme or Vacherin, we recommend your own culinary journey to beautiful Switzerland, or simply to your favorite delicatessen.

The wood engraving, published in the Schweizer Chronik by Johann Stumpf in 1548 depicts cheese making centuries ago in Switzerland.
Overleaf: Switzerland presents itself here as a skiers' paradise near Untersaess/Klosters in Canton Graubünden.

Bacchantian Delights From Valais to Ticino

Good food requires a good wine. Switzerland can offer both. Even if her wines are not as famous as the white wines of the Rhine slopes or the red wines of France – since Switzerland does not have the rare Riesling stock or the climatic conditions necessary for the best quality – all in all Swiss wines reach a remarkable quality. Along these lines, we should also mention that Swiss wine is rather modest and it is not considered necessary to praise it with a plethora of additional ribbons, prize seals or creative confusion. The Swiss can save themselves these methods of fighting for market shares, which have almost gotten out of hand in some wine-producing countries, because the nearly one million hectolitres of wine which are produced annually, on average, are consumed almost solely domestically.

Swiss viniculture is very old and probably was of some importance during the Roman rule over the Helvetians. In any case, a small twig of wood which definitely came from a noble vine was found in the remains of a Roman army camp near Brugg and estimated to be about 2,000 years old. In the first centuries AD, the Romans spread wine-making across their northern territories and wine was intensively grown in the Rhône valley at that time. In the 9th century AD, Swiss wine experienced a first climax. Especially the monasteries appreciated the grape juice, not just for religious purposes, and increasingly began to prefer it to their home-made beer.

As the standard of living rose in the late Middle Ages, wine became affordable to the common people. In order to meet the wildly rising demand, vineyards were established everywhere, even in regions which were as unsuitable for the vines as any-

The stone houses of Engadine are famous for their sometimes magnificently painted, or sgraffito decorated, houses. This richly painted house in the Engadine – House Clagluena – is to be found in Ardez. The story of the fall of Adam and Eve was painted in 1647 and the decoration of the double bay window followed in 1770.

DVMENG.CLALGVNA
IVZI ET ION CLAV.ET IA
CHEN SEIS FILGS A: 1647.
QVID SISQVIDFVERISQVIDERIS
SEMPR.MEDITERIS.
SIC MINVS ATQVE MINVS
PECCATISSVBYCIERIS.

one could imagine. It is said that in those days wines were made in Uri and Schwyz that were so sour that they had to be stored for thirty years before they became at all potable. If not steadily, the popularity of wine continued into the beginning of the industrial age, since now the common laborer could also afford his glass of wine. As a consequence, this development led to the establishment of ill-considered quantities of vineyards, even in poor locations and with vines of inferior quality. That simply could not continue, and after the largest vineyard area of 34,380 hectares was registered in 1884, wine making declined sharply. The consumers were not satisfied with the mass-produced quality; small and very small vineyards were no longer economical to operate, and vine diseases which were brought in in the mid-19th century did the rest.

After numerous adulteration scandals crowned all the other difficulties, the disillusioned consumers returned to their old, time-honored favorite friend, to beer. Following this unsteady phase in Swiss wine making, the way was paved for a stable future by the wine statute of 1953. The cultivated acreage has stabilized around 13,000 hectares and is concentrated in the best locations. The most suitable varieties are grown, and a very careful and controlled treatment of the wine secures a high, consistent quality.

Let's turn for a while to the Swiss wine-growing areas in more detail. Western Switzerland produces the largest share of Swiss wines, about three-quarters of which are white and one-quarter red. The most exceptional and most widely used variety of grape is the Gutedel, which ripens early, brings good yields and offers a stable, fresh and tasty wine. By the way, with this word Gutedel we encounter a

Wine tasting in the cellar of the "Office des Vins Vaudois" in Lausanne. Here the wines of Vaud are allowed to mature in wooden kegs with artistic paintings. Most predominant in this region are white wines, and among them the Chasselas grape is dominant. This grape is also known as Gutedel. All wines from this grape produced in Vaud may use the registered name "Dorin".

Overleaf: Swiss vineyards are always surrounded by magnificent scenery, as here in the vineyards above the Spiez Castle on Lake Thun.

remarkable characteristic of Swiss wines and their names. In Valais you simply drink a *Fendant,* in the regions around Lake Geneva and Lake Neuchâtel you encounter a *Chasselas,* in Vaud the *Dorin,* in Neuchâtel and on Lake Biel the *Twanner* and *Schafiser* – and it's always the same wine from Gutedel grapes, of course with variations in taste which are influenced by location, climate and treatment. If, for instance, you encounter a *Johannisberg* on the wine list, it is not the famous Riesling from the Rheingau at an incredibly low price, but rather a Sylvaner wine from Valais.

Western Switzerland can offer some notable red wines since the noble Pinot Noir and gamay grapes find ideal conditions here. Especially well-known and appreciated is the Valaiser *Dôle* which is nothing more than a harmonic, strictly controlled blend of both sorts.

As we said, descriptions of locations are rarely found; in general only the region and the grape are listed on the label. There is perhaps an exception in Vaud, where there are some famous, more limited growing areas with vineyard locations, such as Aigle, Yvorne, Dézaley or La Côte. Here, too, the Gutedel grape dominates the scene with a proportion of four to one. In the cantons Neuchâtel and Bern, the wine connoisseur will encounter a peculiar type of wine, the so-called *Sternliwein,* or Star Wine. It is a white wine, sometimes also Pinot Noir as a rosé, Œil de Perdrix (in Neuchâtel) which is taken from the yeast and bottled before the end of the fermentation process. This allows some of the natural carbon dioxide to remain in the wine and when poured into the glass the famous star appears. By the way, the same is true of some Pinot Noirs in the region around Maienfeld in Graubünden. Towards Eastern and Northern Switzerland, the vineyard acreage decreases because of natural conditions, although the region around Lake Zurich has, for example, some very nice wines to offer. In older times, vineyards were extensive here and made up more than ten times the current acreage. And in the chronicles of 1865 a so-called "best of the century" wine is praised in verse:

Frost and snow
Boys in the lake – what a show
Blooming vines, ripe cherries – quite gay
It all happened the same month of May.

More than half the grapes of this region are Pinot Noir grapes, but the variety Riesling × Silvaner (Riesling times Sylvaner) is well represented with nearly thirty percent. Especially interesting, and actually somewhat curious, is the fact that this variety is widely sold in Germany under the name Müller-Thurgau. And it was this Dr. Hermann Müller from the canton Thurgau who was able to create this tough hybrid, about one hundred years ago, which is said to produce a "tasty, pleasant, very fruity and usually mild" wine. In sunny Ticino we find almost exclusively red wines in a total area of 900 hectares, not exactly a lot. In almost every restaurant or grotti in Ticino, you can order "mezzo litro di nostrano", which means nothing more than half a liter of "ours". The Nostrano is usually pressed at home and is made of several grape varieties – whichever grapes grow in the vineyard – and the wines which come to the table as Nostrano are surely among the most palatable and least adulterated wines.

In Graubünden, Veltliner is consumed with the specialty of the canton, Bündner Fleisch (air-dried beef, thinly sliced). This red wine is a blend of Chiavennasca, Pinot Noir and Merlot grapes and is not at all identical with the variety of the same name from Austria. The wine production of the Italian Valtellino, which belonged to Graubünden until 1797, is almost exclusively exported to Switzerland. Veltliner is also produced in the southerly Val di Poschiavo.

Of course, we can only touch on Swiss wines in this book. There are many more from all the wine-growing regions, some rare and old specialities, and I can do no more than give some good advice: always drink the wine from the grape which grows locally. That is where it will taste the best. Swiss wines are honest, almost always well fermented and tasteful. In short – as lovely as the landscape in which they grow.

Grapes usually grow best at an altitude between 100 and 400 metres. Switzerland has, however, some wine-growing regions which are particularly blessed climatically such as in Valais, where grapes are grown as high as 800 metres above sea level. At such an altitude it is, of course, most important to protect the vines from frost. The result shows in this graphically attractive photograph.

Food and Drink Keep Body and Soul Together

Food plays a basic rôle in the cultural and social development of people, of course. This is expressed in many sayings, proverbs and customs. Documents and findings from earlier times also tend to prove this.

"Eat and drink, child; food and drink are the best cure for a heartache," said an old man tried by life to his crying child at a wake. The common proverb in Munstertal, "after one has eaten and drunk, Satan is no more" is a conspicuous counterpoint to ascetic religious maxims. The proverb, "The way to a man's heart is through his stomach" is known to all of us, and peasants and craftsmen often say, "A man works as he eats."

Today, popular thought still assumes that food influences the whole person, that one is what one eats. There is doubtlessly a close relation between the belief of the cannibal who thinks that he will assume the strength of his victim by eating his flesh and the opinion of the worker or farmer who thinks that he gets no strength from mutton or veal, which rather make him tired, or the mother who fears that her child will become estranged to her if it is fed the milk of an animal or another woman.

"Chi mangia erba, dvainta bescha" (he who eats grass will become a sheep), says a proverb from the Engadine which expresses a folk belief – not only

Food and drink are, of course, always the focal point of the many Alpler festivals and markets in Switzerland. The upper row shows scenes from an Alpler festival on the Moosalp in canton Vaud, lower left a scene from the market in Vevey and lower center and right, pictures of the famous Zibelemaerit (red currant market) in Bern, which is held every year at the end of November.

Overleaf: The good old farm living-room-quintessence and pride of country culture. Coziness and warmth are radiated by this living room in the Geigenmuehle in Neerach, canton Zurich.

figuratively. The wild men or *Fanggen* of the Alpine folk tales were as agile as mountain goats because they fed on the milk of mountain goats. Even today, mountain goat hunters from Graubünden believe that one must drink the blood of a freshly killed goat in order to gain the sharp eye and quickness of·the animal. Superstition and scientific speculation of the era of enlightenment are intertwined in the idea expressed by travelers of the 18th century that eating cheese and ziger (whey) made the inhabitants of certain Alpine regions melancholy.

Communal meals were of much greater importance in times gone by than they are today because of the belief in the positive effects of the food. In some regions, eating an apple or a slice of bread together (as in the Roman custom of *Confarreatio*) was considered a legal ritual of engagement. In other regions, the wedding couple had to ceremoniously eat from the same bowl. Drinking from the same glass binds not only those in love but is also an old ritual of brotherhood and friendship. This lives on, somewhat faded, in our modern custom of drinking from the same glass "to health", as was customary in the nineteenth century, or in toasting, where the glasses at least touch.

Eating and drinking was and is one of the most important socially induced and socially supportive customs in everyday life and at celebrations. The feeling of belonging arises today in most cases even without the belief in the cohesive effect of the food, simply due to physical proximity of the group at the table and due to the vitalizing effects of food and drink. The closest social unit, the family, meets daily to eat together. According to good Swiss custom, the servants and other employees are a part of this unit. Especially in old farming families and middle-class families, the communal meals follow a customary order or even a ceremonial ritual. This is emphasized by the custom of saying Grace, which in rural areas fell into disfavour only in the second half of the last century. Everyone had his place at the table, which was determined by his position in the household. The common bowl, which forces steady, considerate eating, at which each person has to keep to his own corner, was the symbol of community dining. When the head of the household put down his spoon, the communal meal was over. The community meal out of one pot has, by

the way, experienced a renaissance in our times thanks to the wide-spread popularity of fondue meals.

Characteristic of the general dissolution of the old-fashioned community spirit was the custom of giving everyone his own plate, which originated with the upper classes. Not until the eighteenth century were tablecloth and napkins introduced.

Even today, the custom of a guest or a new member of the household having to eat and drink something upon entering the house lives on in rural and middle-class families. This friendship had to be responded to, regardless of whether or not one was hungry or thirsty. Here, eating becomes pure social custom and acceptance ritual. Refusal of the food or drink is considered a refusal of the community group, as an insult. Thus, paying visits in rural areas can become an ordeal because of the danger of overeating.

At weddings, baptisms or funerals, the larger family circle meets at table. The wake originally was not only intended to unite the living, but also to create communion with the deceased. In Prättigau in Graubünden, a place was symbolically set for the deceased. *Palorma* (per l'orma = for the soul) was the name of the funeral dinner in Engadine, which was done away with because of excesses. These days, people drink a shot of schnaps *Palorma* when the cow is slaughtered by the butcher in the farmyard.

Larger social groups assemble on special occasions for a banquet, dinner party, donation dinner or sacrificial dinner, where the amount of food consumed usually far exceeds normal needs. The debouchery on such occasions is quite acceptable and traditional. Certain feasts were originally held to magically influence the fertility of the crops during the coming year by abundant eating. In this connection, we should not, however, forget that the diet of most people right into the nineteenth century was extremely scanty. No wonder that people lost control on the few festive occasions where food and drink were served in abundance. One especially charming description of the eating and drinking habits of those times is handed down to us by the Pastor Albert Bitzius from Lutzelfluh in the Emmental, who is better known to us as Jeremias Gotthelf:

"As it grew dark, the harvest feast was to begin, but it was not easy to get the people to come. Vreneli, red as a crab from baking all day, finally became angry and said that those stupid people had been licking their fingers all day up to their arm-pits and beyond, but no one wanted to be responsible, no one wanted to agree; so it was impossible to get started and to proceed, and then in the morning it would be impossible to get anyone away from the table, they would sit there as if burned into or nailed onto their chairs. Finally someone would still be missing who should have been dragged in by his ears."

"There was meat soup with saffron in several bowls on the table, into which the bread had been so thickly cut that a person could have knelt on a bowl. Then came beef, fresh as well as dried, bacon, and sweet slices of dried apples. Three kinds of cake, stacked high, and a few bottles of wine, each as big as a keg, were standing on the table, and there was little room for everything so that the servants often did not know where to put things down. Sparrows in millet must feel great, but they still do not know how things are on a harvest table which groans under its load, and beneath which it is impossible to get your legs to hold still because they want to get out and see what smells so deliciously up there.

"But it was not good enough for everyone in this room. Elisi and Trinette did not want to associate with the coarse people and the coarse food. In a side room, a special table was set, and on it was red wine, fish in a sauce and sweet peas and roasts of veal and pigeon, baked fish, hams and cakes, fancy rolls instead of bread, a small pot of sweet tea for the fanciers who like tea and desserts, which the hostess had been saving since her last baby. The children went from table to table, were more wonten at each mew table and finally, too full of food and drink, had to be carried off to bed like depraved little devils. Elisi and Trinette described to each other what they could stand to eat, wrinkled their noses at everything, saying what this did to them and that, this caused gas and that caused nightmares; that affected their eyes and this the ears; this caused constipation and that diarrhea. Oh well, but it was sure worth it!"

"All the while they ate some of this which caused constipation and some of that which caused diarrhea (it must cancel each other out), and their drinking habits did not reveal anything about their poor disposition."

Food and drink is also a customary bonding element for the farm community, which may not come together as a dining party, but in which certain tastes cause a common bond based on age-old traces in origin and habit. For many people, the specialties from home, like those mother used to make, provide great elements of ties to home – which really manifest themselves to a person in different surroundings confronted with different foods. The disparaging proverb of city-folks, "What the peasant doesn't know, he won't eat" has an element of truth, in that the person who has the strongest bonds to home also has the strongest bonds to home cooking, which is the only food he can enjoy and which really satisfies him. Eating habits and the tastes they form are a part of one's very being and it is really an insult to be asked to eat something strange, or one feels sorry for the wealthy guests in the hotels who are there to eat the garbage of the world called "delicacies". While a farmer from Graubünden may only feel up to beginning his daily chores after a breakfast of "Türggeribel" (corn which has been blanched and then fried), the farmer from the central plateau even today believes that corn is only fit to be fed to the hogs and the chickens. Up until the early 18th century, the beginning of the great revolution in agriculture and other fields, we have to picture Switzerland as being divided into the ancient economic and historic two or even three dietary regions, which correspond generally to the agricultural divisions. In the central plateau, an old agricultural region, the original breakfast dish was gruel, the evolutionary predecessor to bread. This ancient food of the grain farmers is mentioned historically as oat or wheat gruel, or in corresponding soups, as the morning meal. It is still eaten in some regions, for example, around Lucerne and in Basel-Land, as oatmeal or porridge. The food of the herdsmen of the northern Alpine regions presented a clear contrast to the food of the farmers in the central plateau. Up to one or two hundred years ago, the diet in this region was largely based on milk or milk products. Instead of bread, lean cheese was eaten with fat cheese. In central Switzerland, the morning meal consisted of milk and ziger cheese or "Zigersueffie" (fresh, white whey), often with dried fruit added as a substitute for bread. These days we can find the old-fashioned herdsman food, especially "Sueffi" for breakfast with dried fruit ("Schnitz") on the morning table only in Unterwalden, a canton with a particularly well preserved animal husbandry tradition.

In some regions, for instance, in Appenzell and to some extent in Glarus, people ate neither corn nor potatoes for breakfast, but rather *café au lait* with bread and butter, as in the city. This coffee with plenty of milk, the "reverse coffee", which attracts the attention of the foreigner as a Swiss peculiarity, has also become part of the urban breakfast.

The central and southern Alpine zones never had a real herdsman food, as would have been appropriate to the mixture of ancient Alpine agriculture and livestock raising. Various kinds of cereal, often of millet, which continues to be grown in the Berner Oberland, and gruel and flour dishes *(Ribel, Tatsch, Maluns)* have survived sporadically in some regions to the present day as traditional breakfast dishes, especially where Alpine agriculture has not completely disappeared. This picture of the three natural zones in Switzerland, which also determine the dietary habits, has considerably changed since the upheavals which began in the 18th century.

The changes in the world economy brought a rapid decline of agriculture, not only in the Alps but also in the plateau, and this naturally caused modifications in the basic Swiss diet.

Potatoes were first and most extensively grown in the central plateau, and the fried potatoes *(Proetleti, Herdoepfel,* Zurich; *Praegleti Haerdoepfel,* Basel; *Braeusi,* Aargau; *Roeschti,* Bern) spread south towards the Alps and from Bern westerly towards the French speaking area, where the fried potatoes from Bern, under the name *Roeschti,* supplanted the older peasant breakfast of soup. Potatoes for breakfast have taken over in the course of the last century in the herding country of the northern Alps, and in the central Alpine regions.

This frontier of potato dishes, moving down from the north is confronted in the central Alpine regions with the corn dishes, in the form of polenta (Ticino), Ribel (Graubünden, Rhine Valley) or corn soup (Valais). It can be followed through Vorarlberg and the Tyrol as far east as the Eastern Alps.

Although surrounded by neighbours who prefer to eat flour based dishes, pasta or spätzle, the Swiss are great potato fans. There is probably no other country on earth that has so many different, ingenious potato recipes as Switzerland. Our pictures on the left show modern potato planting in Wilen, Thurgau, and the traditional method in Cimalmotto in Ticino.

Above: A mountain farmer in Engadine with bundles of barley on his back, descending into the valley. Barley is very robust, and its short gestation period and moderate moisture requirements make it very suitable for mountain growing. Especially in Engadine and Graubünden, much barley is grown, and some very appealing recipes using this grain originate there.

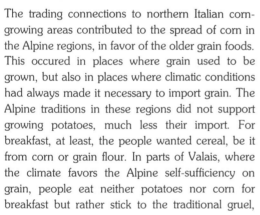

The trading connections to northern Italian corn-growing areas contributed to the spread of corn in the Alpine regions, in favor of the older grain foods. This occured in places where grain used to be grown, but also in places where climatic conditions had always made it necessary to import grain. The Alpine traditions in these regions did not support growing potatoes, much less their import. For breakfast, at least, the people wanted cereal, be it from corn or grain flour. In parts of Valais, where the climate favors the Alpine self-sufficiency on grain, people eat neither potatoes nor corn for breakfast but rather stick to the traditional gruel, which is sometimes replaced by meat broth for the morning meal. This is also a common habit in the Valais colony of Bosco Gurin in Ticino, as is polenta. In a few regions of Ticino, especially in the southern tip of Switzerland, as in the West, around Geneva, the traditional breakfast soup *(Süpa, Soupe)* has been able to hold its own. This soup, as in the neighbouring French and Italian areas with similarly varied growing conditions, is a hearty vegetable soup with all sorts of ingredients. This was also the traditional morning meal in the vineyard country of Vaud along Lake Geneva. And how nourishing it was!

Exterior symbols of Swiss hospitality – artfully worked restaurant signs invite you to food and drink.
Appenzell – a small village back in 1547 is famous for its excellent cheese.

Customs and Festivals

Each Swiss canton frequently has reason for festivals of any kind, based on old traditions. Old customs are very clearly reflected here, and, naturally, almost all of these festivals include food and drink. We would like to describe a few of the most famous customary festivals in detail. In Ticino, housewives are freed of kitchen chores for at least one day during the pre-lenten season. They can take a carefree stroll along the piazza, watching others do the cooking for them. The cooks are local butchers and restaurant owners, and the food – prepared gratuitously for the whole population according to old customs – is an aromatic, saffron-yellow *risotto.* In another pot sizzle the *Luganighe,* spicy pork sausages with garlic. The giant copper kettles are set up on the piazza the day before. They are filled with water, beef and bones, and log fires are built under them. The aromatic fragrance of the meat broth, which tickles the noses of passers-by, tingles anticipation of the risotto. The cooks, who stir the pots the next morning with their long wooden ladles, are strong men. For, in order to cook a risotto successfully, it has to be stirred untiringly and, at the same time, very carefully, from beginning to end over a very hot fire. Drawn by the tempting smells, old and young stream onto the piazza at midday. Everybody gets his serving of saffron rice and a sausage. To crown the meal, there is a glass or two of wine. On improvised tables and benches, a merry feast begins, which eventually turns into a real folk festival. The *Banda communale* plays dance music for the adults, and the children amuse themselves on the *Schlaraffenbaum,* a long, smooth, well-soaped pole with ham, sausages, whole chickens and panettoni hanging from the top, which the indefatigable climbers try to reach.

Now let's turn to another festival and while travelling from the South to the North, from the Catholics in Ticino to the Protestants in Basel: on the Monday before Shrove Tuesday, a few minutes before four in the morning, all the lights go out in the inner city of Basel. Hundreds of piccolos pipe, hundreds of drums reverberate. They all begin with the same march, the *Morgestraich.* That's the term the people of Basel use for the call to their carnival. Overhead swing the brightly painted lanterns casting their pale light in an almost eerie fashion onto the shadowy figures of innumerous spectators on the sidewalks. Then the sky, too, gets brighter and the freezing, costumed and uncostumed people stream into the warm inns for gruel, cheese and onion pie. In the afternoon, the long march of the Cliques begins, which, each group independently, wind their way along the official routes through the city. Through the artistically designed costumes each discloses its *Sujet,* the object selected for ridicule in the Swiss- or Baseler year just gone by. In the market square waits the "Comité", the jury. Along the way, the Cliques distribute from their floats mimosas, oranges or chaff and their *Zeedel,* long, colorful stripes of paper which describe the subject of their clique in witty, imaginative dialect verse. The transition into the descending night moves as slowly as the onset of dusk. More and more people fill the inns, where *Schnitzelbängler* circulate later so that they can present pointed, aggressive scenes in picture and verse. Individuals appear in costume and poke fun at politicians, friends and aquaintances in the sassy local dialect. The old costume balls have nearly died out. Instead, the Cliques, groups and smaller groups wind through the narrow streets of the inner city.

And the last of the revellers do not go home before morning, almost twenty-four hours after the strike of four. But not for long. On Tuesday, the streets belong to the *Guggenmusiken,* musicians who play as loudly and as out-of-tune as possible on a variety of brass and percussion instruments. And the whole thing is repeated on Wednesday, from afternoon until well into the night. Then it is finally over – until next year.

Next, let's take a side-trip into western Switzerland and pay a visit to the *Vignolage:* in the first weeks of March of the new year, high up in the villages St. Luc and Chandolin in the Val d'Anniviers, one dwelling after another is closed. The inhabitants descend to the valley; it is time to go to work in the steep vineyards around Siders. The whole village moves out, complete with mayor, pastor and teacher. It no longer takes place according to the old

This shop in Lugano, the largest city in Ticino, with its front open to the street, clearly radiates southern European, Italian atmosphere. The metre-long imitation sausages are well-designed to attract customers.

Ever since 1808, carnival in Basel has begun precisely at four o'clock in the morning of the Monday before Shrove Tuesday with the ringing of St. Martin's bell. Then the lights go out in the inner city, and the command, "Attention-Morgestraich-forward-march!" comes from every corner. The Cliques with Drummeli (drums) and Piccolos (fifes) start to move. Grotesque masks, colorful costumes and artistically designed lanterns take over Basel and its citizens for the next three days.

customs, with heavily laden donkeys that carefully carried the small children packed into saddle bags, because these people know how to appreciate and utilize technological advances. These folks from the Val d'Anniviers, self-sufficient and bound to the soil, lead a nomadic life between home in the vineyards, the parish, and the Alpine cabins on the *Maien-sässen*. On the Saturday after St. Joseph's Day, the Anniviards gather to do the work in the community vineyard. It is a big day, the day of the *Vignolage*. Led by two pipers who tease shrill, bright sounds from their wooden instruments and, accompanied by the heavy beat of the drum, the lively group of vintners, laden with tools and provisions, moves out to the community vineyards. This festive meeting with the vineyard dates back to an old custom from the 14th and 15th centuries. Before they begin their tasks, the men kneel on the soil to be worked, to pray for God's blessing, knowing that one single night of frost can ruin the work of a whole year. The mayor allocates the work by groups: cutting out the old shoots, tying the new trellises, turning over the soil, applying the fertilizer. The favorite people of the day are the *procureurs*. They are responsible for drink. The persons who untiringly fill the glasses are the *Gardes-Champêtres*. Three musicians cheer the workers with old, traditional melodies. To the beat of the drum, the heavy hoes dig deep into the earth, the vine clippers click short and sharp. When the last ray of sun has disappeared over the near-by mountains and the rich smell of freshly turned soil fills the air, a thanksgiving prayer rises heavenward

once more. Then the people relax and give in to the delicious wine from the vineyard and their hopes for the coming harvest. Led by the merry musicians, the small group makes its way homeward to Muraz/ Siders in the twilight. In addition, there are many other similar festivals all over the country which we cannot describe here in detail.

Mountain farmers are self-sufficient people, bound to the soil. They often lead a nomadic life between the Alpine cabin and their houses in the valley. With bag and baggage, they go up to the meadow in early summer not to return until the Alpabfahrt (trip down from the meadow) in the fall. Of course, these days such trips provide a welcome opportunity to put on an attraction for the tourists.

One of the old Swiss customs is shot putting. This sport, using smooth rocks, is often part of rolicking popular festivals. Left: Burning the "Böögg" is a wide-spread custom in the Alemannic regions. Its purpose is to remove the useless and left-over remainders of Winter to make room for Spring and fertility. Especially magnificent is the burning of the Böögg in Zurich, as part of the Sechselaeutens – the ringing of the six o'clock bells. On the third Monday in April, six o'clock in the evening on the dot, the doll of cotton and straw is burned at the stake on a gigantic bon-fire. Numerous fire-crackers are hidden in the doll, which provides fun especially for the children. Superstition has it that the stability of the Böögg predicts a good or a bad year. The spectacular event is preceded by a colorful parade of the guilds and children.

The masks and costumes have an old and variegated tradition in German Switzerland. Especially charming are the New Year's Kläuse (Santa Clauses) from Urnäsch in the Appenzeller Country, which are impressive with their

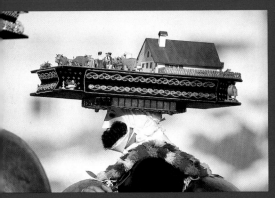

rich and artistic "plate hoods". The masks usually have a unique, quiet smile. The Kläuse from Urnäsch appear on December 3 and again on January 13, a date attributable to the Julian calendar.

What is Swiss Cuisine?

Now we are slowly coming to the actual topic of this book. If you leaf through international cook books, you will either find no Swiss recipes at all or very few of them, fewer than, for example, those for specialties from countries such as Portugal, Sweden or Russia. Swiss cooking usually comes to an abrupt halt after roesti and fondue. Some international gastronomic experts claim there is no such thing as a separate Swiss cuisine, or they consider it unimportant. One reason for this might be that in the many excellent tourist restaurants and hotels in Switzerland, French *haute cuisine* is the order of the day. But that is true for all hotels with an international reputation all over the world, and if everything were that simple, there would be practically nothing left but French cuisine. Yet, the Swiss could claim in this regard that they cultivate this cuisine with real love and perfection. But, honored as the Swiss may feel when their achievements in the kitchens of the famed restaurants are praised as the "famous Swiss cuisine" by enthusiastic outsiders this definition nevertheless, is not correct.

So let's look for the original, native, home-grown Swiss cuisine. And we'll be successful as soon as we leave the restaurants which cater to the tourist trade and search for small country inns, look around in traditional Swiss households or visit the many local festivals in the country-side. Here we find, from one canton to the next, a really very rich and original cuisine which can be justly termed Swiss.

It is frequently said that the eating habits of the Confederates are a mosaic of the cuisines of neighbouring Germany, France, Italy and Austria. I must take exception to this notion for it is not even a half-truth. This could perhaps apply to Ticino at best, where doubtlessly, quite a few things were taken over from the neighbour to the south because of language and geology. But only certain things, and those selectively. Where are the many varieties of pasta or pizzas in Ticino? Where in the other parts of the country and cantons do we find the Austrian sweet desserts, the well-seasoned recipes from the French provinces with their variety of vegetables, where can we find the spaetzli or the knoepfli from the northern neighbours in Swabia? None of these dishes have been able to penetrate the Swiss cuisine at all or only just a little.

Through the very example of the overwhelming excess of noodle-pasta-spaetzli- and nockerl-eating neighbors, the stable independence of Swiss cuisine has proved itself. It is built upon a broad foundation of potatoes and nowhere else in the world are there so many different and ingenious potato dishes in such a small area as in Switzerland.

Certainly, borders do not only separate, they also unite. Certainly, many foreign cooking secrets have crossed over into Switzerland, but many, too, have crossed out, as, for example, Baron Eugen von Vaerst says in his Gastrosophie: "The best confectioners in the whole world, who can be found in all big cities in Europe and abroad, come from Graubünden. There, these people we see from Mexico to Petersburg in grey jackets and white aprons, own great stone palaces." So there – and nothing has changed in the quality of Swiss chocolates and pastries even to the present day.

The influence which the returning Swiss soldiers are supposed to have had on the eating habits of their native country has doubtlessly been overestimated. Only long-term foreign occupations have truly left culinary traces in the home-land, not, however, the Swiss mercenaries returning from foreign soil. As paid soldiers in the service of the Kings of France, they would hardly have taken part in the splendid banquets in the palace of Versailles. They got the same primitive, unimaginative and monotonous rations as all those at the lower echelons of war making. And if they got a chance to devour a *Gueggeli* (chicken) as bounty after a battle, they had more important things to do than write down the recipe to take home. Not to mention the fact that mercenaries in those days could hardly read and write. So they did not bring any recipes with them, although they did probably bring the bright red pants as guards of the King of France, from which the Engadiners, pragmatic as they are, made their beautiful bright red native costumes.

Certainly, there are exceptions. Swiss legionnaires probably brought back the Spanish Soup which the country boys might have concocted there in the field pots out of all ingredients within reach and so popular today. Somehow, Spanish rolls also got into the country, which especially the Badeners could bake so crisply. When the first railroad line in Switzerland opened from Baden to Zurich on August 9, 1847, the Zurichers, too, could finally enjoy this specialty fresh from the oven for breakfast. The railroad was, therefore, lovingly christened "Spanish Roll Train". All in all, however, the guest appearances of Swiss soldiers abroad have at best only touched the Swiss cuisine, but not really influenced it.

It exists, as we have seen and will see in the course of this book – the real Swiss cuisine. It originated like every regional cuisine in the world, namely, from local fruits, garden vegetables and the products of local domestic animals. At one time that was very little, since Switzerland was a poor country before "The Discovery of the Alps", as a book by Roy Oppenheim is titled. From the very little available to eat, the housewife had to use all her skill and imagination to add variety to the menu. And what she managed to conjure up out of milk, cheese, bread, corn, millet, fruits, and later, potatoes, is amazing and full of variety – it is doubtlessly the foundation of the real Swiss cuisine!

The Swiss love good food as well as sweet tidbits on the side and William Tell's son surely would have preferred to eat his apple rather than balance it on his head for his father's target practice.
Overleaf: This magnificent pillared house with the ornamentally decorated round gable dates from 1698 and can be found in Trubschachen in canton Bern. It isn't difficult to imagine that turning in to this Bear Inn will be an architectural as well as culinary experience.

Alpler Macaroni

Älplermagrone

This dish from Uri – one of the few based on noodles without any potatoes, added, used to be eaten on Sundays and holidays. The food on weekdays was even simpler. A warm dinner would consist of a small amount of fried Alp cheese (which today is appreciated again as a welcome change from the ordinary as neither plain nor cheap). If there was enough time, one of the men would cook up a *Fenz*, a mixture of butter, flour and milk. A kind of snack was, and still is, *Dickete*, milk curdled with rennet.

6 cups milk
1 tablespoon salt
1 pound macaroni (4 cups)
1 1/3 cups mountain cheese (Bergkäse) or Sbrinz,
shredded (6 ounces)
1/2 teaspoon coarsely ground black pepper (or to
taste)
8 tablespoons butter
2 onions, sliced
3 cloves garlic, chopped

Bring milk and one tablespoon of salt to a boil. Add the noodles and cook over low heat until done, stirring occasionally. The noodles should absorb enough milk so that the dish is still moist (if necessary, add more milk). Empty the noodles into a pre-heated bowl, mix in cheese and pepper. Top with onions, which have been sautéed in butter, and garlic cloves. Serve with fresh salad. In Nidwalden, Älplermagroni is prepared with equal amounts of macaroni and potatoes (peeled and diced). Dried apple slices are traditionally served as a side dish.

Fried Apples

Apfel Bröisi

Bröisi means about the same thing as *rösti*, fried potatoes. But in this case it is the apples from the sky and not those from the earth which are fried. An old proverb says, "Bread alone is not enough, for simple bread with nothing else results in a flat belly – and anybody who tries to do anything in that condition will get the yellow pest." The yellow pest probably referred to hepatitis, and this proverb was directed at those people who would gladly collect as large a paycheck as possible for as little work as they could get away with.

1 pound stale French bread or rolls
2 1/4 pounds tart apples
4 tablespoons butter
4 tablespoons sugar
6 tablespoons fresh butter

Slice the bread as thinly as possible. Peel apples, remove core, slice thinly. Heat butter in a skillet, add bread and sugar and toast until crisp, turning constantly. Add the sliced apples, mix well and continue to fry, turning constantly, until the apples are soft. Top with the fresh butter and let it melt. Serve immediately. The bread should not be soft – it really tastes right when it is toasted crisply. If you like, sprinkle with sugar and cinnamon. The original beverage is, as with so many Swiss recipes, café au lait.

Apple Pie

Apfelkuchen

Crust:
1 2/3 cups flour (9 ounces)
1 teaspoon salt
8 tablespoons butter
2 tablespoons water
1 cup almonds, peeled, ground (3 1/2 ounces)
1 3/4 pounds apples (28 ounces)
juice of one lemon
3 tablespoons butter
1 tablespoon sugar
1/2 teaspoon cinnamon

Filling:
2 tablespoons butter
1 teaspoon starch
1 1/2 cups cream
2 tablespoons sugar
1 tablespoon vanilla-flavored sugar
or equiv. vanilla flavoring
2 eggs
1 egg yolk

Blend flour with salt and sift onto a kneading board. Knead diced butter into the flour until crumbly. Add water a little at a time and knead well. Chill the dough in the refrigerator for half an hour. Line the bottom of 10 inch (26 cm) springform pan with the dough and sprinkle with peeled, ground almonds. Then put the apple slices, which have been mixed with the lemon juice, on the crust in concentric circles and brush with melted butter. Bake in 350° F (180° C) preheated oven for 15 minutes and sprinkle with sugar and cinnamon. Bake ten minutes longer. When the apples are almost soft, add the filling. To prepare the filling, melt butter in a pan. Blend in cornstarch, add cream and mix well but do not boil. In a bowl, beat the eggs with the sugar and vanilla until fluffy. Add the cornstarch mixture from the pan a little at a time. Pour over the pie in the oven. After another 15 minutes' baking time the filling will be nearly firm. Sprinkle with a little sugar and top with a little melted butter. Leave only top heat on (broiler) to brown the sugar lightly. Sprinkle with powdered sugar and serve while warm.

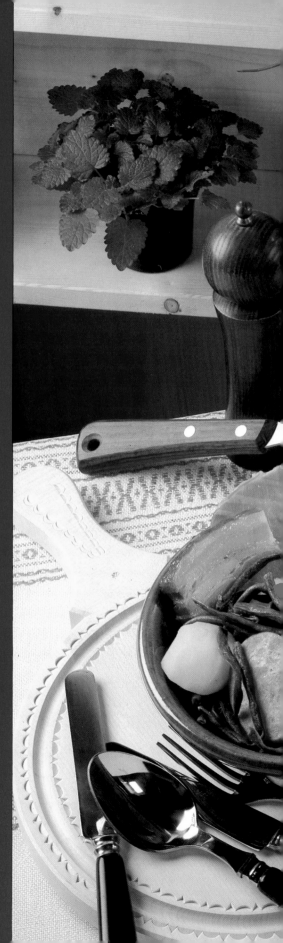

Plate à la Bern

Berner Platte

There are probably as many Plates à la Bern as there are inhabitants in the canton Bern. The meat or sausages can be supplemented or substituted according to fancy or availability. Just as popular with this famous Swiss dish are green beans in place of or in addition to the sauerkraut.

1 tablespoon cooking oil
1 onion
2 lbs sauerkraut
1 cup white wine
1 cup water
1/2 pound smoked bacon
1 smoked pork rib chop
12 ounces well-marbled braising beef
2 pounds medium potatoes
salt
1 tablespoon flour
1 tart apple with skin and core
1 small Berner Zungenwurst (tongue sausage) or country style pork sausage

Heat oil in a pan, sauté the finely chopped onion, add sauerkraut, heat for 2 minutes and then add wine and water. Add bacon and smoked pork chop, parboiled beef and let simmer, well-covered, over medium heat. After thirty minutes, place peeled potato halves on top of sauerkraut, sprinkle with a little salt and replace cover. Potatoes and meat will be done after another 40 minutes. Carefully remove potatoes from the pan and place them in a pre-heated bowl. Then remove the meat, carve into serving-size pieces and keep warm. Sprinkle flour over the sauerkraut, grate the apple directly into the kraut and stir thoroughly. Pile the sauerkraut into a bowl, cover with meat and sausage slices, garnish with potatoes. Serve with mustard.

Pears and Mashed Potatoes

Birre und Stock

If an overnight frost freezes the apple and pear blossoms on the trees in Thurgau, there won't be much left for the fruit growers to do for the rest of the year. From this region around Lake Constance comes this rather unusual looking but very tasty recipe. Cider is very important in this region. As an old-time Thurgauer says: "It is worse to be without hard cider than to be homesick!"

2 pounds potatoes
3 pounds pears
3 cups water
1/2 cup white wine
3/4 cup sugar
1 cinnamon stick
grated rind of one lemon
1 clove, whole
1 1/2 tablespoons butter

Prepare mashed potatoes from the 2 lbs potatoes. Scrub pears, quarter, remove cores, stems and blossom ends. Add water, wine, sugar, cinnamon stick, lemon peel and clove to a pan and slowly cook the pears till juice begins to thicken. Before serving, alternatively put in a serving bowl a layer of hot, freshly made mashed potatoes, then a layer of hot pears, covered with 3 spoons full of the pear syrup, then another layer of potatoes and pears, until everything is used up. The top layer should be mashed potatoes. Top with hot browned butter. Serve with the traditional café au lait. Or make a bigger meal of it by serving it with braised meat, blood sausage and a dry white wine.

Central Swiss Bean Pot

Innerschweizer Bohnentopf

"He is as welcome as a hail-storm in the bean-patch," they say in the country when unexpected or undesired company drops in. "He's in the beans," means someone is distracted and isn't really concentrating. These proverbs indicate how concerned people used to be about the bean harvest. Beans were especially prized as a summer vegetable because they are so versatile. Well-suited to drying, they were also found on the table in winter.

8 ounces mutton
9 ounces smoked neck of pork
1 tablespoon cooking oil
2 pounds green beans
9 ounces carrots
salt
1 sprig summer savory
2 pounds small, new potatoes

Cut mutton and pork into small serving-size pieces. Heat the oil in a skillet, quickly brown the meat, add the cleaned and stringed beans and the cleaned and thickly sliced carrots. Add salt to taste and hot water. Top with summer savory and cover the vegetables with the small, peeled, lightly salted potatoes. Cover. Simmer well covered one hour, or until potatoes are done. They should retain their shape and not fall apart. Serve with hearty dark bread and a light red wine or Pinot Noir.

Onion Pie

Bölledünne

"They may make you cry a lot, but you still can't get along without them!" Even if bitter tears are shed while peeling, there is hardly a household in which onions are not used in the kitchen in some way.

Crust:
1 1/2 cups flour
6 tablespoons butter
1 tablespoon water
1/2 tablespoon vinegar
1 teaspoon salt

Filling:
4 large onions, thinly sliced
2 tablespoons shortening or oil
1/4 cup bacon, finely diced
1 1/2 tablespoons flour
1 cup milk or cream
2 eggs
salt

Place flour in a bowl, cut small pieces of butter on top of it and rub together with your hands. Add water, vinegar and salt and knead until smooth. Cover and let dough rest for 15 minutes in a cool place. Line a well-greased pan or large pie plate with dough which has been rolled out not too thinly. Peel onions, slice thinly and sauté in oil and finely diced bacon. Take from heat, dust with flour, stir well. Add cream, eggs and pinch of salt and mix until thick. Spread over crust, top with flakes of butter if desired and bake in medium oven about 40 minutes. Serve hot to warm with a glass of hard cider if you can get it. A dry white wine will do just fine.

Sweetbread Custard Pie

Brieskuchen

Briesmilch is the milk of a cow that has just delivered a calf. For about one week the mother cow produces this milk which is especially rich in protein, vitamins and minerals. Naturally, the Swiss, with their traditional, world-famous dairy industry, recognized the value of such milk and developed a few recipes using it. The recipes described here come from the Emmental and are very old. The first version is salty, the second sweet.

1 1/4 cups flour
3 eggs
2 cups Briesmilch
1/2 cup cream
1 pinch salt

Mix flour with the eggs, milk, cream and salt and beat well. Pour into casserole and bake at medium to low heat about 40 minutes.

1 1/4 cups flour
5 eggs
2 cups Briesmilch
1/2 cup cream
1 pinch salt
3/4 cup sugar
lemon peel and vanilla to taste
Prepare and bake pie as above. Serve either version with café au lait.

Tipsy Apples
with Ice Cream

Bsoffni Öpfel mit Is

Legend has it that around the year 900, Wendilgart, the wife of Udalrich of Buchhorn, sought refuge in the cloister of St. Gallen. This lady had an insatiable longing for goodies. With time this became too expensive for the cloister kitchen. Wendilgart prayed to the Holy Mary and asked for the fervently desired sweets – and, behold, the Holy Mother sent down a couple of apples. These were, however, so sour that Wendilgart cried out with dismay. "O Holy Mother of God, if Eve had gotten such a sour apple from the serpent in Paradise, she would never have been tempted!"

1/4 cup dried apples, minced
1 heaping tablespoon raisins
1/2 cup calvados (apple brandy)
2 tablespoons mango chutney
4 tablespoons, strained low-fat cottage cheese
lemon juice
1/2 teaspoon cinnamon
2 tablespoons powdered sugar
dash ground pepper
4 large apples (Gravensteiner if available)
1 lemon
2 tablespoons sugar

Soak minced, dried apple pieces and raisins in Calvados for at least 12 hours. Then blend well with mango chutney, cottage cheese, some lemon juice, cinnamon, powdered sugar and pepper. Pare apples, rub with lemon juice, cut off a lid and carefully remove core. Place in hot 465° F (240° C) oven for 2 minutes in baking dish. Then fill with above mixture. Replace the apple lids, sprinkle with sugar and bake for about 15 – 20 minutes. Serve with apple ice cream flavored with Calvados. Vanilla ice cream will do as well.

Graubünden Platter

Bündner Teller

The dried beef from Graubünden has become world-famous, but even at home this quintessence of international hors d'œuvres is usually made in factories these days. But it is still much better than the many imitations around the world, which usually have nothing more in common with the original Bündner product than the name. Bündner Fleisch is produced from very tender, finely textured and well-marbled pieces of the rump muscle. It is rubbed with a mixture of pepper, juniper berries, herbs and salt. Then the meat is dried for several months (in factories much faster thanks to the use of air blowers!) in the spicy mountain air of Graubünden, if possible above 1.800 metres (approx. 5.500 feet) in altitude, during which time it loses about 50 percent of its original water content.

Bündner Fleisch and/or Mesolcina
cornichons
tomatoes
whole rye or wheat bread
pepper

Slice Bündner Fleisch and/or Mesolcina (a ham seasoned with garlic from Graubünden and the Ticino valley) razor thin. ("It should be possible to read the newspaper through ist," a connoisseur once said.) And arrange attractively (loosely rolled if desired) on a wooden plate. Garnish with cornichons (little sour pickles) and tomato wedges and serve with whole rye or wheat bread, freshly ground pepper and a Veltliner or white wine.
Some fanciers of Bündner Fleisch swear that the meat tastes even better finely diced. Why not try both variants!

Tripe Soup

Busecca

Swiss minds are widely split about tripe. In a poll, every other person asked remarked that tripe is dreadful. Nevertheless, about 3,000 tons are consumed every year in Switzerland, which indicates that one of two Swiss is an admirer of this delicacy.

1 onion, chopped
2 cloves garlic, chopped
1/4 cup bacon, diced (2 ounces)
1 tablespoon olive oil
2 1/2 cups bouillon or white wine
2 stems leek, sliced
1 celery root or several celery stalks, sliced
3 tomatoes, sliced
3 carrots, sliced
1/4 pound green beans, sliced
1 cup green peas
1 small head cabbage, sliced
1 pound (beef) tripe, cut in strips
1 teaspoon salt
marjoram
sweet basil } *one pinch each*
rosemary
saffron
2 tablespoons tomato paste
3 potatoes, peeled and diced
9 cups water
Sbrinz or Parmesan cheese, shredded

Chop onion and garlic and fry in oil with the bacon, add bouillon or white wine. Clean and slice all vegetables (except potatoes). Take 9 cups water, add the onion, bacon, garlic and vegetables. Bring to boil and simmer about 1 hour, then add tripe, season. Add tomato paste and simmer another 15 minutes. Then add potatoes, peeled and diced, and simmer lightly, covered, 20 minutes. Serve with shredded Sbrinz or Parmesan cheese sprinkled on top.

Mountain Omelette

Cholermues

A typical herdsman's dish from the mountains of the cantons Nidwalden and Obwalden. The herdsmen produced the ingredients themselves and knew how to use them economically but cleverly. There was nothing worse than fraud, nothing worse than wasting milk and other foods – and this is still true today in the Alps. The sociologist R. Weiss reminds us in this connection of the "ghost herdsmen" who, as punishment, have to spend night after night collecting every spilled drop of milk and make cheese from it.

6 tablespoons flour
3 eggs
1 3/4 cups cream or milk (or half and half)
1/2 teaspoon salt
butter

Prepare a rather thick paste from the ingredients. Let stand a while. Bake omelette in hot butter until the bottom is golden brown. Then turn and immediately break up into pieces. Bake until all pieces are lightly browned. Sprinkle with sugar and cinnamon if desired.
Serve with applesauce or stewed pears.

Baked Rabbit

Coniglio al forno

We discovered this baked rabbit in Agarone near Locarno. French influence can be detected in this relative of the hare, for our neighbours to the north-west are particularly fond of rabbit. In the kitchen they differentiate strictly between wild rabbit, which is prepared as poultry, and the domestic rabbit, which is the one used here. Rabbit is very tender, has no strong flavor of its own, is low in calories but rich in protein and minerals. It is considered to be a white meat, but that should not stop us from serving a Ticino red wine with it.

1 young rabbit, about 2 to 2 1/2 pounds
salt
pepper
1/4 cup oil
8 tablespoons butter
2 tablespoons sage, finely chopped
2 tablespoons rosemary, finely chopped
4 juniper berries
1/2 cup white wine
1/2 cup Marsala

Cut the oven-ready rabbit into large pieces, salt and pepper it and brown in butter in a casserole in the oven. After about half an hour, add sage, rosemary and juniper berries with some white wine and Marsala. Baste often with the remaining wine and Marsala (if liquid evaporates and the meat is left high and dry, add some warm water). The rabbit should be nicely browned and crispy, not too dry, not too moist. Roast a total of about 1 1/2 hours at 430 – 480° F (220 – 250° C). Serve with polenta, rice or mashed potatoes and a red wine from Ticino. As a very compatible supplement we recommend apples or pears braised in wine.

Perch Filets in White Wine

Eglifilets in Weisswein

(6 servings)

In Switzerland perches, which can weigh up to 1 kilogram, are called "Egli", and their filets are highly favored for various dishes.

2 pounds fresh perch (Egli) filets
salt
pepper
lemon juice
Worcestershire Sauce
flour
4 tablespoons butter
1 1/2 cups heavy cream
1 cup dry white wine
herbs
6 ounces (1 1/3 cups) fresh mushrooms,
thinly sliced
parsley, chopped

Thoroughly clean perch. Rub with salt, a dash of pepper, lemon juice and some Worcestershire Sauce, lightly flour and sauté in butter. Meanwhile, heat cream and wine and gently boil about 5 minutes. Season to taste with salt, pepper and herbs. If you drink a nice white wine with your fish, something which is always to be recommended, it is advisable to use this same wine for the sauce, too, since the quality of the wine affects the quality of the sauce. Clean the mushrooms and slice thinly. Arrange the perch filets on a warm platter. Top with raw mushrooms and pour the boiling sauce over it. Sprinkle with chopped parsley. Serve with rice, thin noodles or boiled potatoes and a salad.

Duck's Liver on Oyster Mushrooms

Entenleber auf Austernpilzen

The oyster mushroom (Pleurotus ostreatus) prefers trunks of poplar or beech trees which have been split open by lightning or wind. The brownish gray fungus adheres to the trunk, with hardly any stem to speak of, sometimes several metres up. This picture reminds of oysters clinging to pilings. When young and fresh, the oyster mushroom is very tasty. In recent years this mushroom has been commercially grown and is increasingly available in stores.

Juice of half lemon
1 teaspoon olive oil
salt
pepper
1 or 2 large oyster mushrooms
1 slice of duck's or goose liver about 3/8" thick,
roughly 2 ounces flour
2 tablespoons butter
vinegar (black currant or wine vinegar)
dry sherry

Prepare a marinade from lemon juice, olive oil, salt and pepper and marinate the mushrooms in it for a few minutes. Remove and gently sauté in its own juice on both sides for short time, keep warm. Lightly salt and pepper the liver with freshly ground pepper and dust with flour. Fry on both sides in butter until golden brown. Remove from pan, keep warm. Pour some of the fat from the liver over the mushrooms. Add a few drops of black currant vinegar or a good wine vinegar to pan. Add a little dry sherry and boil down the juices by one-half. Arrange the liver on the mushrooms and top with the sauce. Serve with a glass of Fendant or Chablis.

Trout Filets à la Zug

Zuger Felchenfilets

Mousse:
5 ounces filet of Felchen or other trout
2 1/2 ounces filet of sole
salt
herbs
Tobasco Sauce
2 egg-whites
1 cup cream

Filets:
12 filets of Felchen or other trout
salt
white pepper
lemon juice
4 tablespoons butter
6 tablespoons chopped onion
parsley
chives
tarragon
marjoram
thyme
white wine
3 tablespoons butter
2 tablespoons flour

Cut up fish filets for the mousse and marinate in salt, herbs, Tobasco Sauce and egg-whites. Purée the marinated fish and fold whipped cream into it. Spread out the 12 Felchen filets, rub with salt, pepper and lemon juice. Spread the mousse about 1 inch thick on the filets, roll up and fasten with toothpicks. Place onions, finely chopped herbs, white wine and the fish rolls into a buttered pan. Cover with aluminum foil and lightly simmer in the oven 5 – 8 minutes. Melt 3 tablespoons butter in a small pan. Blend in 2 tablespoons flour until smooth, but do not brown. Add liquid from fish and stir, obtaining a white sauce. Enrich with a little cream. Season with salt and pepper and boil down to desired thickness. Pour sauce over trout. Serve with rice and salad.

Rhine Trout in Champagne with Fine Herbs

Rheinforelle in Champagner mit feinen Kräutern

The Swiss rivers and lakes are still the hunting ground for river and salmon trout, but the tremendously increasing demand for these fish can only be met by raising the American Rainbow Trout on fish farms. If you ever have the chance to get really fresh, wild trout, don't fail to take advantage of this delight!

1 lake or river trout 2 to 2 1/2 pounds or
2 smaller stream trout, 1 pound each
10 tablespoons (abt. 6 ounces) butter
2 bunches finely chopped parsley
fresh dill
sweet basil
summer savory
1 clove garlic
1 cup champagne
salt
pepper
juice of half lemon
Worcestershire Sauce

Clean fish and wash thoroughly. Cream butter until fluffy, add finely chopped parsley, herbs and garlic. While stirring constantly, add champagne and season with salt, pepper, lemon juice and Worcestershire Sauce. Slash trout diagonally, wrap air-tight in aluminum foil, together with the herb mixture, leaving room for the trout to expand under heat. Place in pre-heated 480° F (250° C) oven for about 20 minutes. Serve with boiled potatoes and green salad. Crown the meal with a cool white wine from Lake Constance or Schaffhausen.

Fruit Bread à la Glarus

Glarner Früchtebrot

For St. Nikolaus's Day, *Samichlaus* in Switzerland, December 6, fruit breads and Lebkuchen ginger-breads are baked all across the country.

3/4 ounce live yeast or equivalent in dry yeast
3/4 cup milk
3/4 cup water
4 tablespoons butter
3 cups flour
1 teaspoon salt

12 ounces dried pears
6 ounces dried Italian prunes, pitted
2/3 cup raisins (3 1/2 ounces)
3/4 cup (3 1/2 ounces) walnuts, coarsely chopped
1 tablespoon kirschwasser (cherry brandy)
2 1/2 tablespoons sugar
1 teaspoon cinnamon
1 pinch ground cloves
1 pinch nutmeg blossom
1 egg yolk

Dissolve yeast in lukewarm milk, add melted butter. Sift flour with the salt. Add milk to flour. Knead until smooth, allow to rise in covered bowl in a warm place about one hour. Soak pears and prunes over-night in cold water. Cook in the soaking water about 20 minutes, drain off water and put fruit through the meat grinder. Add coarsely chopped nuts, to fruit mixture. Add raisins (which have been soaked in kirschwasser) sugar and spices. Knead mixture into one-third of the dough and form two narrow loaves. Roll out remaining dough, cut into two rectangles and wrap around the fruit loaves. Fold the ends under and place on metal baking sheet with the seam on the bottom. Prick several times with a fork. Allow to rise in a warm place one hour. Brush with egg yolk and bake in pre-heated 340° F (170° C) oven for about one hour.

Caramel Crème

Gebrannte Creme

In earlier days, Caramel Crème was occasionally served for dessert on Sunday. This was the absolute "pièce de resistance" of Sunday dinner for the children, it was the dessert they had waited for all week – or longer. On weekdays they were lucky to get an apple or some dried fruit. Thus, this crème became the ultimate symbol of Sundays, holidays or birthdays.

2 egg yolks
7 tablespoons sugar
3 tablespoons starch
2 1/2 cups milk
1 tablespoon water
pinch of salt
1 cup cream

Beat egg yolk and 2 tablespoons sugar until very light. Separately mix cornstarch with 1/2 cup milk. Heat remaining sugar in a pan until it is brown and begins to foam, add water, then remaining milk and a pinch of salt. Heat until sugar has dissolved. Add cornstarch solution and bring to a boil. Add to egg-sugar mixture while beating with a wire whisk. Return everything to pan, bring to a boil and immediately remove from heat. Cool.
Serve with whipped cream.

Zürich Veal

Zürcher Geschnetzeltes

What Beef Stroganoff is to the Russians, Zürcher Geschnetzeltes is to the Swiss. Both dishes, one filet of beef, the other filet of veal, have conquered menues around half the world. As for our *Züri Gschnätzlets,* the following comment is frequently true: often imitated, never matched!

1 1/4 pounds veal cutlet
flour
4 tablespoons butter
1 small onion, finely chopped
1/2 cup white wine
salt
pepper
1/2 cup cream

Slice veal into narrow julienne strips, dust with flour. Heat butter in a skillet and sauté the onions until tender. Add the meat and stir for about one minute over high heat until it has taken on a whitish color on all sides. Add white wine, salt, freshly ground pepper and cook another 2 – 3 minutes. Thicken with the cream. A few tips for the well-travelled gourmet: Experts remove the meat from the pan after one minute and let it drain on a sieve. A sauce is made from the broth in the pan, and the cream and the meat are added again just before serving. By the way, in Zurich macaroni and apple sauce used to be served with this, while today rösti (fried potatoes) constitute the prevailing side dish. There are opposing gourmets who insist that a fine rice is the only proper accompaniment. But it's high time to wish you bon appetit for your *Züri Gschnätzlets!*

Cheese Soufflé

Gratin Montagnard

Browning under the broiler (au gratin) not only makes a dish more nutritious, it also improves its appearance. Au gratin means: browning the top of an almost cooked dish in a heat resistant dish under the broiler. Since we eat with our eyes as well as our palates, such dishes really should have a delicately browned crust. To prevent the food from burning while browning, we usually add a little liquid such as cream, bouillon or a thickened sauce.

1 quart milk
salt
2 tablespoons butter
6 tablespoons cream of wheat
1/2 pound Gruyère or Emmental (Swiss) cheese,
thinly sliced
ground nutmeg
4 egg yolks
4 egg whites

Bring milk, salt and butter to a boil, stir in cream of wheat and heat over low heat to a thin paste. Add pinch of nutmeg. Thinly slice the cheese, stir into the hot mixture until cheese has melted. Remove from heat and cool. Then add beaten egg yolks. Fold in stiffly whipped egg whites. Fill a well-greased soufflé dish two-thirds full with mixture. Bake in pre-heated oven a good half-hour. Serve with a green salad and a cool fruity white wine from Valais, for example, a Bonne Côte.

Elderberry Preserves

Holunder-Latwerge

The black elderberry (sambucus nigra) is a bush growing up to twenty feet high or a tree with gray-ish-brown bark. The sweet-smelling blossoms appear in large, flat clusters. The berries are round, about 1/4″ in diameter, black with a blood-red juice. Elderberry plants grow wild in Switzerland from the flatlands up to 1.500 meters altitude in deciduous forests, forest edges and in groves, thriving on wide-ly varying soils. The berries contain an ingredient which reduces fever and induces perspiration. The berries can be eaten fresh or made into preserves or syrup. The expression "Latwerge" means some-thing like cooked fruit in dialect and originates from the Greek *Ekleikton,* which is the designation for a medicine which can dissolve in the mouth. Our Elderberry Preserves can be considered a kind of natural medicine because of their contribution to good health, but they really taste delicious and can be used to garnish omelettes, as a spread for bread or for making the Valaiser dish Sii (see recipe p. 192).

2 1/2 pounds elderberries
1 1/2 cups sugar
nutmeg
ground cloves

Remove berries from stems and wash. Heat over low heat with very little water until they burst. Pass through a sieve, then boil slowly with 1 1/2 cups sugar for each 2 1/4 lbs strained berries until mix-ture slowly drops in large pieces from a spoon. A dash of nutmeg or cloves added towards the end of cooking improves the taste.

Dandelion Blossom Honey

Honig von Löwenzahnblüten

The dandelion has many names. In various Swiss dialects it is called *Chrottepösche, Chueblueme, Souwblueme*. In Germany it is also called *Pusteblume* (Blowing Blossom) because of the flighty seeds. At the slightest breeze the seeds detach from the stalk and drift away like little parachutes. The dandelion has a 4″ – 12″ (10 – 30 centimetre) long taproot. Its long, narrow leaves, tooth-edged both sides, were probably the reason for the dangerous-sounding German name *Löwenzahn*. The English name's derivation from the French "dent de lion" = Lion's tooth, sounds just as ferocious. The plant blooms from late June until October and grows in Switzerland from the flatlands up to an altitude of 10.000 feet (3.000 meters). The dandelion prefers rich, moist soil. An old home remedy is a tea of dandelion leaves and roots. It is supposed to be good for liver diseases, kidney problems, hepatitis and other diseases.

1 basket of dandelion blossoms
sugar

To prepare the honey, first collect a basket of dandelion heads. Pluck out the yellow petals and barely cover them with water in a large pan. Simmer for 15 – 20 minutes. Strain through fine-meshed sieve over a large bowl. For each quart of liquid, add 2 lbs of sugar, and boil until the liquid reaches the consistency of honey. This takes 2 – 3 hours. The syrup is then filled into pre-heated bottles and tighly sealed. It makes a tasty spread for bread or a nice addition to tea on a cold winter day.

Filet of Veal à la Fisherman

Kalbsfilet Fischerzunft

This recipe comes from Schaffhausen and in a way presents a companion dish to Zürcher Geschnetzeltes. It is a modern creation of the international Swiss cuisine, but the use of filet of veal pays tribute to the country which, probably justifiably, claims to have the best veal in the world.

8 fresh artichokes
juice of half a lemon
1 scallion
4 tablespoons of butter
1 pound mushrooms, thinly sliced (abt. 3 cups)
1 cup white wine
1 cup cream
1/2 cup bouillon
salt
1 tablespoon green peppercorns
summer savory
1 1/4 pounds filet of veal (cut into 8 equal serving-size pieces)
butter

Clean the artichokes. Remove the hearts, which are the only part to be used, rub them with lemon juice and cook in salt water until just soft. Chop scallion and sauté in butter. Thinly slice mushrooms and add to the scallion, sauté. Add wine and allow to thicken. Add cream and bouillon and bring to a light boil. Season to taste with salt and pepper. Sprinkle chopped summer savory over sauce. Lightly salt meat and brown lightly, about one minute on each side, in butter. The medaillons should be rosy pink on the inside. Arrange artichoke hearts on a platter, fill with sauce, top with slices of meat. Serve with rösti (fried potatoes) or noodles and a dry white wine.

Potatoes au Gratin

Kartoffelgratin

When the potato plant was brought to Europe from South America, it did not have a good reputation. For a long time people thought this curious plant with the whitish-yellow blossoms might be pretty to look at but was not suitable for eating purposes. The *Tartüffeln*, as these truffle-shaped tubers were called because of their shape, were considered to be poisonous and many claimed that eating such a devil root would cause people to become stupid. Thank goodness that this is not the case, for where would the Swiss be without their potatoes – or with potatoes that made them stupid! This dish from Fribourg is so good you probably won't care.

1 3/4 pounds potatoes, raw, sliced
salt
pepper
nutmeg
1 1/4 cup shredded Gruyère
1 cup milk
1 egg
butter

Grease casserole with butter. Alternate layers of potatoes, seasonings and cheese. Mix milk and egg and pour over potatoes. Bake about one hour in the oven. Serve with fresh salad and a glass of white wine.

Potato and Cheese Casserole

Kartoffel-Käse-Auflauf

A great chef, Johann Rottenhöfer, wrote about the potato more than one hundred years ago, "They are probably the most important of all the vegetables given to man by the Creator. They appear on the tables of Kings and Emperors and in the hovels of the beggars. The culinary arts have achieved an amazingly wide variety of potato dishes." The Swiss have paid particular attention to this, and there is hardly another country on earth which can rely on such a wealth of experience on how handle solanum tuberosum.

2 pounds potatoes
salt water
4 tablespoons flour
4 egg yolks
1 cup shredded Gruyère
1 cup shredded Sbrinz
salt
nutmeg
2 cups milk
4 egg whites
2 tablespoons butter

Wash, peel and dice potatoes, cook until soft in salt water. Drain, let dry and pass through strainer. Meanwhile mix flour, egg yolks, cheese, seasonings and milk. Add potatoes, then fold whipped egg whites into other ingredients. Bake in a well-greased baking dish, top with flakes of butter, beginning in a slightly pre-heated oven and gradually increase the heat. Serve with lamb's lettuce or water cress.

Cheese Rösti

Käserösti

A rösti (fried potatoes) is worth its plate! Around Bern, pottery making has a long tradition. Especially pretty roesti plates are made primarily in the workshops in Langnau and Heimberg – ornamental decors and motifs from nature and everyday life are typical. Often old wisdoms and religious proverbs as well as charming and witty jokes are found on the plates, for example, "When our maid is done – she eats the meat and we the bone." Cheese roesti exist in other cantons, of course, especially in Uri, Appenzell, in Valais and in Fribourg, wherever cheese making enjoys a particularly long tradition.

2 pounds potatoes, boiled in their skins
1 1/2 tablespoons butter
1/2 cup diced bacon and/or sliced onion
2 oz. sliced Gruyère (5 – 6 slices)

Peel and shred potatoes. Heat butter in skillet, add potatoes, diced bacon and/or onions and sprinkle with salt. When a crust begins to form on the bottom, turn the roesti, top with cheese slices and press down. Cover tightly so that the cheese will melt nicely and bake until golden brown. Serve onto a plate. Cheese roesti goes especially well with bratwurst (fried sausage) and browned onion rings. Such a hearty cheese roesti can make an exciting meal of its own, however, if served with a lot of green salad and wine or beer, or, if you prefer, café au lait.

Chestnut Casserole

Kastanien-Eintopf

In an old chronic from 1658 we can read, "Virginity can be compared to a Kestine, if it gets too close to the fire it pops!" Kestine is, of course, our good Kastanie, or chestnut. The German word Kastanie derives from the Latin *Castanea*. In the Swiss dialect this word *Kestine* has become *Cheschtene*. Chestnut trees thrive magnificently in the mild climate of Ticino, and its fruit, which is very nutritious, was an important part of the diet in the past. Maroni are a delicate variety of sweet chestnuts. The fruits of this tree have been appreciated in Switzerland for at least 5.000 years.

1 pound edible chestnuts
1 medium head cabbage
1 pound potatoes
2 cups diced bacon
4 luganighe or 4 large pork sausages
1 cup bouillon

Slash chestnuts and boil about 10 minutes. Peel. Separate cabbage into leaves and blanch about 5 minutes. Drain well. Peel and cube potatoes, dice bacon and cut sausage into thick slices. Line a casserole with half the cabbage leaves, fill with mixture of potatoes, bacon, sausage slices and chestnuts. Pour in bouillon, cover with remaining cabbage leaves. Cover casserole and bake in preheated oven at about 350° F (180° C) for a good hour. Serve with a red wine from Ticino, for example, a Merlot.

Cherry-Bread Cake

Kirschenbrottorte

One characteristic of cooking in former days was the desire to cook as imaginatively as possible with the few ingredients available and to find new combinations of foods. It was also necessary to be economical with food. Part of this effort was using up all left-overs. Stale bread was, for instance, the basis for the bread cakes, which have a wide variety of fillings. The citizens of Basel are still masters in the preparation of sweet dishes and desserts, as this recipe proves.

6 stale rolls
2 cups milk
4 eggs
2 tablespoons sugar
1 tablespoon vanilla-flavored sugar or vanilla
flavoring
1 1/2 cups grated almonds (5 1/2 ounces)
1 cup cream
2 lbs black cherries
2 tablespoons kirschwasser (cherry brandy)
grated peel of one lemon
1/4 teaspoon cinnamon
powdered sugar

Break rolls up into small pieces, cover with lukewarm milk and after a few minutes pass through the strainer. Add the 4 egg yolks, sugar, vanilla-flavored sugar, almonds, cream, kirschwasser, lemon peel and cinnamon, then blend in the cherries. Carefully fold in the stiffly whipped egg whites. Turn into a greased 10″ (26 cm) springform pan and bake in a pre-heated oven at medium heat about 40 – 50 minutes. After cooling, remove from pan and dust with powdered sugar.

Cherry Cake à la Zug

For nut layers:
4 egg whites
8 tablespoons powdered sugar (4/5 cup)
1 cup grated hazelnuts (3 1/2 ounces)
1 tablespoon cornstarch

For sponge-cake layers:
3 eggs
3 tablespoons water
5 tablespoons powdered sugar
3 tablespoons flour
3 tablespoons cornstarch
1/4 teaspoon baking powder
grated peel of half lemon

For butter crème:
8 tablespoons butter (4 ounces) unsalted
1 cup powdered sugar (9 ounces)
1 egg yolk
4 tablespoons kirschwasser (cherry brandy)

For the topping:
4 tablespoons kirschwasser
1 cup chopped, roasted hazelnuts (4 1/2 ounces)
3/4 cup powdered sugar

For the **Nut layers,** whip egg whites until stiff, blend in half the powdered sugar. Mix remaining ingredients and fold into egg white mixture. Spread two equal layers in a 10″ (26 cm) springform lined with aluminum foil (one after the other) and bake each for 20 minutes at 300° F (150° C.) For the **Sponge-cake** layers, beat the egg yolks with 3 tablespoons water until creamy and stir in 4 tablespoons powdered sugar. Whip the egg whites with the remaining tablespoon sugar until stiff, put on top of egg yolk mixture and fold in the remaining ingredients. Bake in a springform lined with aluminum foil at 350° F (180° C) for 20 minutes. For the **Butter crème,** cream the butter until fluffy, slowly add powdered sugar and egg yolk, then stir in kirschwasser. Spread one nut layer with about one-third of the butter crème, place sponge-cake layer on top and sprinkle with kirschwasser. Spread another layer of butter crème on the cake, place the other nut layer on top of it and spread with the remaining butter crème, cover the top with the nuts and dust with powdered sugar. Criss-cross the top layer.

Basel Goodies

Basler Leckerli

In the beautiful old city of Basel, the so-called Imbergässlein runs down from the Nadelberg to the Schneidergasse. Here is where the ginger bread bakers, nick-named "Lebküchner", used to live. They used ginger (Ingwer) in making their spicy, aromatic products, and the name of the Imbergässlein derives from the name of this spice. The world-famous Basler Leckerli, which can look back on a 600-year-old tradition, were invented here. Basler Leckerli are made without any shortening at all. Over the years, the more economical candied orange and lemon peel have replaced the ginger. You can, of course, use some of this spice for the Leckerli without any problems.

1 1/8 cup honey (9 fluid ounces)
1 1/4 cup sugar
2 teaspoons potash or baking soda
1 shot glass kirschwasser (cherry brandy)
4 tablespoons candied orange peel (2 1/2 ounces)
4 tablespoons candied lemon peel (2 1/2 ounces)
3/4 cup chopped almonds (3 1/4 ounces)
1/2 teaspoon cinnamon
1/2 teaspoon ground cloves
dash nutmeg
4 3/4 cups flour
grease for baking pan

Heat honey in a pot, add sugar until melted and bubbling, allow the mixture to cool. Dissolve potash or soda in kirschwasser and add to sugar and honey. Gradually add orange and lemon peel, almonds, spices and flour, let dough rest overnight in a cool place. The next day, roll out dough about 1/4" thick. Bake on greased square metal baking sheet at 400° F (200° C) about 20 minutes, allow to cool a bit and cut into squares as desired.

Braised Beef à la Merlot

Manzo brasato al Merlot

The Italian name of this beef roast hints at southern European origins, but it really becomes clearly a product of Ticino only, with the Merlot. This red wine grape grows today on about half of all vineyards in Ticino although it was not introduced there until 75 years ago. It proved to be the grape best suited to the climatic conditions in Ticino. Of all the Swiss red wines, the Merlot needs longest to mature, but it keeps the longest and wines from the best years can be stored up to ten years.

2 1/4 pounds beef rump roast, larded
salt
pepper
3 tablespoons oil
3 celery stalks, diced
4 carrots, diced
2 onions, diced
3 tablespoons tomato paste
1 1/3 cups red wine
1 2/3 cups consommée (of beef)
1 bay leaf
2 whole cloves

Rub beef with salt and pepper. Heat oil and brown beef in it. Remove meat. Brown carrots, celery and onion well. Add tomato paste and stir. Add wine and briefly boil. Add consommée, return meat to pan, add bay leaf and cloves. Slowly braise, covered, for 1 to 1 1/2 hours. Strain liquid, season with salt and pepper, bind with a little flour if desired. Pour over sliced meat. Serve with polenta (corn meal) and a glass of Merlot from Ticino.

Basler Carnival Soup

Basler Mehlsuppe

Sometime between February 8 and March 15, the citizens of Basel are attacked by a unique bacterium, the effects of which they cannot resist. It is the Carnival bacterium and it is effective every year for exactly three days, from early morning until late at night. On the Monday before Carnival Tuesday, four o'clock in the morning on the dot, the legendary Morgenstraich begins: Cliques wind through the old town of Basel with *Drummeli* (drums), *Piccolos*, *Stäggeladerne* (artistically painted lanterns on a stick), lanterns on their heads, scary masks and colorful costumes. This spectacular show ends around seven, and then *Mählsupp* and *Zibelewaije* (onion pie) are served to the revellers.

3 tablespoons butter
4 tablespoons flour
1 small onion, finely chopped
4 cups water
2 cups bouillon
salt
pepper
nutmeg
marjoram
grated Sbrinz or Parmesan cheese

Brown flour in melted butter. Stir constantly with a wooden spoon. It is a disgrace in Basel to allow lumps to form or the flour to burn! Add chopped onion and sauté. Add water and bouillon and simmer at least three quarters of an hour. Season to taste with salt, pepper, nutmeg and marjoram. Garnish with cheese and serve.

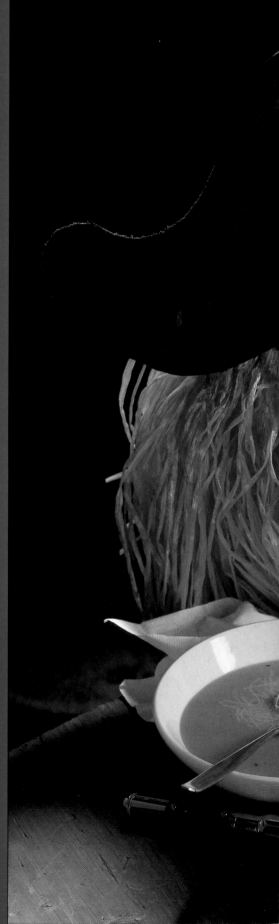

Minestrone

"Take everything at hand, have no regrets, add it all, and the result is a fine *Minestra!*" This soup has been made in our country ever since the earliest days under the name *Manestre*. If *Minestra* can be any kind of soup, then minestrone is always a vegetable soup with noodles.

1/2 cup diced bacon
1 tablespoon olive oil
1 large chopped onion
1 piece oxtail
3/4 cup pinto beans (4 1/2 ounces) soaked
3/4 cup navy beans (4 1/2 ounces) soaked
1 1/4 pounds fresh vegetables, finely diced (e. g. carrots, kohlrabi, cauliflower, leek, celery, cabbage, pears or vary with season)
3/4 pounds tomatoes, peeled
10 cups water
salt
pepper
parsley, chopped
marjoram
sweet basil
tarragon
thyme
bay leaf
1 clove garlic
2/3 cup rice (not parboiled), (6 ounces)
3 cubed potatoes
1 cup elbow macaroni
1 cup red wine
grated Sbrinz or Parmesan

Sauté bacon in oil until transparent, add onion, oxtail, beans, all vegetables and the tomatoes. Sauté for 5 – 8 minutes. Add water, salt and seasonings, bay leaf and crushed garlic. Simmer the soup over medium heat, well covered, 30 – 45 minutes. Add rice, potatoes, noodles and wine and cook over low heat until done. Serve garnished with grated cheese.

Barnyard Scratcher

Mischtkratzerli

Once upon a time there was a comfortable farm, house and barn, nearly inundated with heavily laden fruit trees, gilded by the rays of the setting sun. There was a big compost pile in front, and on top of it, young, white chickens, industriously scratching around, untiringly picking. They were well-fed, not fat, just right – for a dish known and beloved in many variations. It is really important to the flavor of the birds that they are raised in the barnyard. When shopping, look for these country chickens, even if they are somewhat more expensive than the factory-grown variety.

2 broiler-fryer chickens
salt
paprika
herbs
1 tablespoon butter
1/2 onion, chopped
1 carrot, diced
1 celery root or 4 stalks celery, diced
1 leek stem, diced
1/2 cup white wine
1 cup fresh mushrooms, sliced
1 cup cream
1 teaspoon butter
1 teaspoon flour

Quarter chickens, season and fry chickens, in butter over medium heat about 20 minutes. Add onions and vegetables, sauté briefly, add wine and mushrooms. After 5 minutes remove chickens from pan and keep in warm place. Simmer vegetables another 10 – 15 minutes. Add cream, bring to boil, add flour-butter mixture, stir, season to taste and pour over the chickens. Serve with buttered noodles and a cool white wine or rosé (Clevner) from the slopes around Lake Zurich.

Chocolate Mousse

Mousse au chocolat

It may be that this classic dessert did originate in the French *haute cuisine*, but Swiss chefs have enthusiastically adopted it, and they have the main ingredient, chocolate, available right at home in the very highest quality. The Spaniards also contributed to the development of this chocolate foam dessert since they were the ones who discovered the cocoa bean from the Indians in Mexico during their conquests in the 16th century, and the *xocolatl* drink they made from it. Are you one of the many people who sometimes get an insatiable craving for chocolate? This is probably due to the theobromine in chocolate which is a stimulant that sometimes can totally upset your calorie consciousness. But our good chocolate is not nearly as bad as the Viennese physician Johann Franz Rauch maintained in 1772 when he considered chocolate to be the root of all evil!

11 ounces dark, semi-sweet chocolate
2 tablespoons milk
6 egg yolks
6 tablespoons sugar (4 1/2 ounces)
2 1/2 cups cream

Melt chocolate in milk over medium heat. Meanwhile, beat egg yolks und sugar until fluffy. Slowly fold in melted chocolate. Whip cream until stiff and fold into chocolate mixture. Put in a bowl and chill 4 – 6 hours in the refrigerator.

Fondue Neuchâtel

Neuenburger Fondue

Fondue, just as the equally well-known roesti, is, so to say, a Swiss national dish. The diners sit around a table and dip their pieces of bread, which are impaled on a fork, into the melted cheese. During the meal, the fondue is kept lightly bubbling over an alcohol burner (rechaud) with an adjustable flame. The entire party eats out of the *Caquelon,* a heat-proof dish with a handle especially created for this dish. Many fondue experts dip their bread into kirschwasser (cherry brandy) before going into the cheese.

1 clove garlic
2 cups white wine (dry)
4 teaspoons lemon juice
2 1/2 to 3 1/2 cups grated or shredded Emmentaler
(Swiss cheese)
2 1/2 to 3 1/2 cups grated or shredded Gruyère
1 shot glass kirschwasser (cherry brandy)
1 heaping teaspoon corn starch
pepper
nutmeg or paprika
French bread, cubed (not too fresh)

Rub the caquelon with garlic clove, heat white wine and lemon juice in it, gradually add cheese, stirring constantly. Bring to a boil over medium to high heat, then add kirschwasser in which cornstarch has been dissolved. Briefly simmer, then season with pepper, nutmeg or paprika. Take from stove and place over alcohol burner and begin the meal. While eating, stir the fondue with the bread so that it remains smooth. Serve tea, which is gentler on the stomach than white wine, which can, of course, be served as well.

Noodles au Gratin à la Valais

Nudelgratin valaisanne

In our idiom, noodles are good for many a meaning. A mother says to her child, for example, "Just wait till I noodle you," when the child is in for a minor punishment. Or, we really have to feel sorry for someone who has been "noodled" unjustly in life. You'll be a lot more fortunate with this noodle au gratin dish.

12 cups salt water
3/4 pound noodles
1 pound small zucchini, sliced
1 1/4 pounds tomatoes, peeled, sliced
1 tablespoon cooking oil
1 pound lean pork, cut in julienne strips
1 tablespoon flour
2 onions chopped
2 cloves garlic, crushed
1/2 cup red wine
1 tablespoon powdered gravy extract
1/2 teaspoon salt
pepper
1 teaspoon thyme, finely chopped
1/2 cup mountain cheese (Bergkäse) shredded
2 tablespoons butter

Bring salt water to a boil, add noodles and cook about 10 minutes until "al dente". Steam the zucchini and tomatoes in a little water in a separate pan 5 – 10 minutes. Heat oil in skillet, add meat, dust with flour, and brown, stirring constantly. Add onion and garlic and continue browning. Add wine, gravy powder and seasonings. Arrange noodles, vegetables and meat in layers in a greased gratin dish. Garnish with grated cheese and butter and brown 30 minutes under the broiler. Serve with a Valais red wine, perhaps a light Dôle.

Rice Cooked in Cream

Nytlärys

Nytlä or *Nidle* means nothing less than cream. It isn't difficult to recognize *Rys* as rice. This rice dish cooked in cream comes from the Uri Alps. The cuisine of the herdsmen was always, even at its most luxurious, solid and modest. This was because the men could only take such unperishable staples in modest amounts like noodles, rice, sugar, salt, flour, some seasonings and perhaps onions, garlic and dried chestnuts up to their Alpine meadows. But they were often able to come up with astoundingly creative dishes using these simple ingredients.

2 quarts milk
2 teaspoons salt
1 pound (natural) rice
1 cup cream
4 to 5 tablespoons butter
pepper
salt

Salt milk and bring to a boil. Add rice and simmer 15 minutes, stirring occasionaly. Add cream and continue cooking until the rice is done but still moist (add more cream if necessary). Before serving stir in butter and season with salt and pepper to taste. Traditional accompaniments: apple sauce and café au lait.

Peek-in-the-Oven

Ofenguck

There is hardly another natural food which is so well packaged and protected against external influences as the egg. Its porous but still relatively stable shell is air and water permeable but when stored properly, bacteria have a more difficult time entering. The four eggs in this recipe from the region around Zug give the dish an amusing appearance, and the engaging name really stimulates the urge to try it! Such dishes are, incidentally, very suitable for using up left-overs, for instance, if you have a large amount of mashed potatoes.

2 pounds potatoes
4 tablespoons butter
nutmeg
salt
4 eggs
1 cup finely diced ham
1/2 cup bacon, diced
pepper
marjoram
3 tablespoons Sbrinz or Parmesan, grated

Prepare mashed potatoes, add butter and season with nutmeg and salt. Carefully separate eggs without breaking the yolks. Slightly beat egg-whites and fold into potatoes along with the diced ham. Heap the mixture into a buttered casserole, stick the pieces of bacon in the top. Using a moist spoon, make four depressions, spaced evenly about halfway between the edge and the center, and carefully place an egg yolk in each. Sprinkle with pepper and marjoram. Garnish with Sbrinz and bake the Peek-in-the-Oven at about 430° F (220° C) for 10 – 15 minutes, or put under broiler to brown top.

Oven Door

Ofetori

This dish goes through the *Ofentori,* the *Ofentüre* (oven door). And an oven can work wonders. Its heat can transform ordinary mashed potatoes into a golden mountain of culinary delight, laced with browned, well-seasoned pieces of bacon. The Nidwalders drink *Ghürotnigs* (from the dialect for "married"), a mixture of equal parts of sweet and hard cider, with this.

1 3/4 pounds potatoes
1 egg
1/2 cup cream
1 tablespoon butter
3 tablespoons grated Sbrinz or Parmesan
nutmeg
1 cup lean bacon (1/2 lb)
butter

Prepare mashed potatoes and mix well with the slightly beaten egg, cream, soft butter, cheese and a pinch of nutmeg. Put potato mixture in greased baking dish, smooth and shape top with knife. Cut bacon into short strips and stick them into the potatoes so they can still be seen. Top with flakes of butter. Bake in pre-heated moderately hot oven 20 – 25 minutes. The top should be nicely browned. Serve with a big salad.

Char in Sauce Genevoise

Omble Chevalier in Sauce Genevoise

4 perch
3 tablespoons butter
3 scallions
parsley
chives
thyme
rosemary
tarragon
salt
pepper
juice of one lemon
1/2 cup white wine
1/2 cup water
1 lemon
Sauce:
3 tablespoons flour
4 tablespoons butter
liquid from fish
1 cup cream or milk
2 tablespoons white wine
salt
pepper
2 egg yolks

In a casserole, sauté the minced scallions in hot butter until just golden. Add finely chopped herbs and sauté. Wash and dry the drawn fish and season with lemon juice. Place in the casserole, add salt and pepper. Add the mixture of wine and water. Add a little more lemon juice and barely simmer in pre-heated oven about 15 minutes. Remove fish from liquid (but save liquid for sauce) and arrange on a platter with lemon slices. Keep warm. Brown flour in butter, add liquid from fish and stir the sauce until smooth. Add cream and wine, season to taste with salt and pepper. When the sauce begins to boil, remove from heat and stir in 2 egg yolks until smooth. Heat evenly and pour over fish.

Papet à la Vaud

Papet vaudois

2 1/2 pounds leeks
2 small onions
1 tablespoon butter
salt
pepper
1 cup wine
1/2 cup bouillon
1 1/2 pounds potatoes
1 saucisse aux choux*
1 saucisse au foie* (liverwurst)
or 1 saucisson vaudois*
2 tablespoons butter
2 tablespoons flour
1 cup milk
salt
pepper
nutmeg

Wash leeks and cut in pieces about 2″ (5 cm) in lenght. Sauté the chopped onions in butter, add the leeks and briefly sauté. Season with salt and pepper, add white wine and bouillon and simmer covered for 10 minutes. Remove 3/4 cup of liquid from the pan and set aside. Add peeled and cubed potatoes and continue cooking approx. another 10 minutes. Then add the sausages and barely simmer another 20 minutes. Heat butter in a small saucepan, add flour and briefly sauté. Add milk and liquid from the leeks. Season with salt, pepper and nutmeg, simmer 10 minutes and add to the leeks. When serving, remove the sausages, rinse under hot water, prick and serve atop the vegetables. A glass of wine from Vaud, maybe an Aigle or a Dézaley or any good, dry, white wine will complement this rustic dish.

* Note: Where these Vaudoise sausage specialities are not available replace with the "boiling type" hearty country sausages (pork) available in your area.

Polenta

The word *Polenta* is of Latin origin (*Puls, Pultes, Pulmentum*), but was originally not applied to the famous corn meal dish, but to a mixed gruel of various grains, usually millet or wheat. Polenta was the basic food of the Romans. In Ticino, a real polenta is made in this way: someone with lots of time and who has a fireplace with a roaring wood fire and a copper kettle mixes the corn meal mush from the necessary ingredients and stirs and stirs, up to four hours, until he has a fine, flavorful, golden, thick polenta! As simple as the ingredients may be, as difficult it is to present a really perfect polenta to one's guests.

1 pan or copper kettle of sufficient size
6 cups water
salt
wooden spoon
3 cups corn meal, coarse or medium grind

Bring 6 cups water to a boil, add salt and, stirring constantly, slowly add corn meal. Continue stirring, always in the same direktion to avoid lumps. Reduce heat, continue stirring. After 40 – 45 minutes turn the polenta onto a wooden platter. Bring to the table covered with a linen towel, where the steaming polenta is cut with a wooden knife or a thread. A well-seasoned mushroom sauce and a glass of Merlot or other heavy red wine superbly complement the polenta.

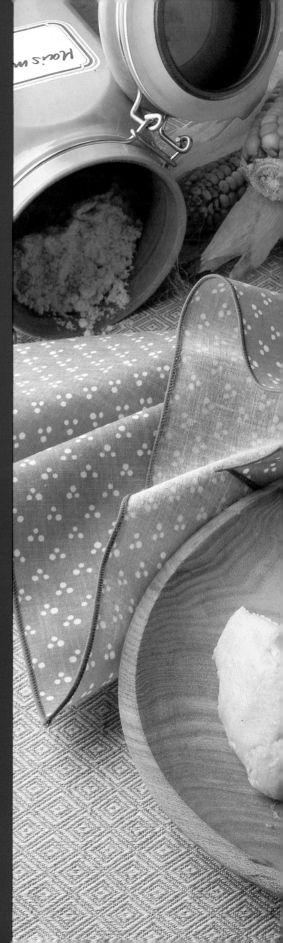

Corn Meal Mush, Beans and Sausages

Polenta, fasöö e luganighe

Corn has been grown in Ticino since the beginning of the 17th century, and it is, therefore, not surprising that polenta is so popular there.

8 cups salt water
3 cups corn meal
1 onion, coarsely chopped
2 to 3 tablespoons oil
2 cloves garlic, chopped
2 tablespoons tomato paste
5 1/2 cups navy beans (soaked overnight)
1 cup bouillon
pepper
salt
dash nutmeg
4 luganighe or Ticino Salsiz*
white wine

Prepare polenta by gradually adding corn meal to 8 cups boiling salt water, constantly stirring with a wooden spoon. Simmer one hour. Meanwhile sauté the onion in hot oil. Add garlic, tomato paste and drained beans. Pour in bouillon, add pepper, salt and nutmeg, and cook the beans, first over medium, then low heat, until done. Place the sausages in a pre-heated cast-iron skillet and add enough white wine to completely cover. Bring to a boil and simmer over low heat until the wine has completely evaporated and the fat oozes out of the sausages. If necessary, add a little shortening and brown the sausages on all sides until crisp. Slice and arrange on top of the beans. Turn the polenta onto a platter or wooden plate, slice and serve with the beans.

* Note: Where this special sausage is not available replace with the "boiling type" hearty country pork sausages available in your area.

Stuffed Apples

Pommes farcies

Around Lake Geneva, clever compositions with ground meat are very popular. Along with the stuffed leeks from Vaud, this recipe for stuffed, baked apples is very original.

12 ounces ground meat (4 ounces each of beef, pork and veal)
1 onion, chopped
1 bunch parsley, chopped
shortening
flour
1/2 cup white wine
3 tablespoons dark raisins
salt
1/2 cup bouillon
4 large apples
4 tablespoons butter

Brown ground meat, onion and parsley in a skillet, with a little shortening. Dust over with one teaspoon flour, add wine, raisins, salt, and bouillon and bring to a boil. Peel and core apples, hollow out from bottom. Arrange next to each other in a buttered baking dish and fill with the meat mixture. Place the removed chopped apple pulp along with the remaining meat mixture in the pan between the apples. Add pieces of butter and bake in pre-heated oven at high heat for 20 to 30 minutes. Serve with boiled potatoes and a cool white wine (from around Lake Geneva).

Beef Soup

Pot-au-feu

"On ne fait pas de rien grasse porée," loosely translated that means, "You can't make bouillon out of stones," meaning that a good piece of meat is absolutely essential to a good beef broth. These days, soup meat is prized all over the world, not least of all because it is easily digestible and only contains a modest amount of calories. It is known by many names: *Pot-au-feu* (pot on the fire), *Bollito misto, Borscht,* and *Siedfleisch,* which earned special honors for the Viennese *Tafelspitz. Gsottnigs* or *Gsottes* in Swiss dialect, that means meat boiled in water until tender.

12 cups water
1 tablespoon salt
1 savoy cabbage, cut in strips
1 stem of leek
1 onion studded with bay leaf and cloves
1 clove garlic
2 1/4 pounds marbled beef
2 soup bones
4 whole peppercorns
1/2 pound carrots
1 celery root, quartered
1 1/4 pounds potatoes, peeled and cubed

Bring salt water to a boil with the vegetables, onion and garlic. Then add meat, bones and peppercorns. The pores of the meat will quickly seal to keep the juices in. Gently simmer about 2 1/2 hours, depending on size and cut of the meat; (it is done much quicker, of course, in a pressure cooker, about 30 to 40 minutes), until meat is tender. Add carrots and celery after the first hour, potatoes about 30 minutes before soup is done. Serve with mustard, cranberries, horseradish sauce and bittersweet Italian plums.

Mushroom Chicken

Poulet Pilzbäggli

One of the most famous gastronomes in Zurich is Emil Bäggli, who is not only a great chef but also a mushroom expert, and so he created numerous dishes with mushrooms. These plants are among the most puzzling of the earthly flora, and their many shapes and colours have always fascinated people. A dish with mushrooms is always a desireable change on the menu of a gourmet. It is, therefore, strange that in a poll conducted in Switzerland on the least liked foods, the mushroom took a thankless second place. This aversion possibly comes from the fact that the edible mushrooms often have deceptively similar poisonous doubles. If you gather your mushrooms yourself, they should always be checked by an expert for edibility.

1 large fresh roasting chicken
or 2 smaller fryers (not frozen)
salt
pepper
1 petit-suisse or Philadelphia cream cheese
10 juniper berries
1/2 pound leaf spinach
1/2 pound fresh mushrooms, thinly sliced
(abt. 2 cups)
4 scallions
fresh herbs (oregano, rosemary)

Salt and pepper chicken inside and out, put cheese and juniper berries inside. In the electric grill, brown until golden brown. Collect juices, and about 10 minutes before chicken is done place the blanched, well drained spinach in the chicken juice in the drip pan and leave with the chicken. Meanwhile, sauté the finely sliced mushrooms with the scallions, season with salt, pepper and fresh herbs (oregano, rosemary). Arrange chicken on a platter and surround with the spinach and mushrooms. Serve with rösti and a dry white wine.

Cream Custard Pie

Rahmfladen

The canton Appenzell has a great pie-baking tradition. These pies come in many versions: fruit, cream, honey, almond or jam pies – and various sizes. And if there is no dessert or pie after a meal, a good Appenzeller joke is sure to be cracked!

Approx. 3/4 pound dough (see recipe on page 72)
2 tablespoons ground almonds
2 1/2 tablespoons sugar
3 eggs
2 tablespoons butter
3 tablespoons flour
1 1/2 cups cream
1 pinch salt
1/4 teaspoon cinnamon
1 1/2 tablespoons raisins
2 tablespoons shredded almonds

Line a pie-plate with the dough and sprinkle with the ground almonds. Beat the sugar with the egg yolks until fluffly, gradually add all other ingredients and finally fold in stiffly whipped egg whites. Fill crust with this mixture, garnish with a handful of blanched almonds, if desired, and bake in medium oven about 40 minutes.

Ramequin

Freely translated, *Ramequin* means cheese pie. The Swiss take this to mean all sorts of dishes with cheese and bread, browned in the oven, which always adds a piquant gratin note to a dish. Suitable cheeses are Gruyère, Emmentaler and Appenzeller, sliced, shredded or grated. Suitable breads are French bread or any left-over, stale bread, cubed or sliced. There are various ramequin recipes, from canton to canton, some of which include diced ham. In Ticino people eat corn with it, which makes the whole thing quite high in calories. In any case, a light white wine or rosé tastes excellent with a ramequin. You can also serve a Mousseux, a special sparkling wine which is popular in Vaud and canton Geneva.

3/4 pound French bread
1/2 pound Emmental or Gruyère cheese, sliced the same thickness as some of the prepackaged types
3 tablespoons butter
2 eggs
2 cups milk
salt
nutmeg
paprika
pepper

Slice bread 1/4″ (1/2 centimetre thick, cheese thinner. Arrange alternately in a greased baking dish, like fish scales, so that the cheese slices slightly extend beyond the tops of the bread slices. Beat eggs with milk, season, pour over the bread and cheese, top with flakes of butter. Bake in pre-heated oven 20 – 30 minutes.

Rice with Chestnuts

Reis mit Kastanien

The Urner had rice, corn and chestnuts in the pantry as early as the Early Middle Ages, since the old Gotthard Pass had put them in the right position for extensive trading with the South. Many local citizens were totally dependent on the traffic across the pass; it gave them work and a livelyhood. They transported merchandise safely and surely from one side to the other. The edible fruits of the chestnut tree, also called maroni, have been used since the 16th century as medicine (diarrhea), but have been able to maintain their popularity among gourmets up to the present day.

1/2 pound dried chestnuts
5 cups bouillon or saltwater
2 cups rice (3/4 pound)
1 1/4 cup Bergkäse or Sbrinz; shredded
(if desired, sauté one large thinly sliced onion in
4 – 5 tablespoons butter)
2 – 3 cloves garlic, chopped
flour

Soak dried chestnuts overnight and cook in the bouillon until half done. Add rice and simmer, covered, stirring occasionally, until done. Before serving, stir in the cheese and garnish with the onion rings which have been sauteed until golden brown in butter. Or, more piquant, sauté the onion rings until golden brown, add chopped garlic, dust over with flour, add bouillon. Bring to boil and pour over the chestnut rice mixture.

Risotto à la Ticino

Tessiner Risotto

Rice has a characteristic unique among grains. Each plant must be planted separately. Also, water plays a much more important rôle than for other grains. The name rice is said to come from Old Sanskrit, where it was *Vrihi*. During its travels west, the name underwent many modifications. The ancient Greek word was *Oryza,* which has become the Italian *Riso*. Italy is also the largest rice-growing area of Europe, and it provides us with the best round-grain rice, which is especially suitable for risotto. Grated cheese is always a part of this dish, in Italy it is usually Parmesan, in Switzerland the terrific Sbrinz. The *Ticinesi* make their risotto with red wine, which gives the rice a unique flavor. Risotto is really a side-dish which goes well with many meat dishes, but many variations and imaginative ingredients turn it into a main dish to serve with fresh salad and a Ticino wine.

1 large onion, finely chopped
3 cloves garlic, chopped
3 tablespoons oil
1 3/4 cups rice (not parboiled)
1 1/2 cups red wine
3 1/3 cups bouillon
2 tablespoons tomato paste
3 tablespoons butter
1 cup Sbrinz or Parmesan, grated

Sauté onion and garlic in hot oil, add rice and cook until glossy. Add wine and boiling bouillon. Add enough tomato paste to give rice a nice red color. Cover loosely and simmer until rice is done. Stir in butter and cheese before serving.

Mushroom Risotto

Risotto ai funghi

Funghi is the Italian word for any kind of mushrooms. The *Steinpilz*, yellow boletus (boletus edulis), is considered king of the mushrooms. Its even, brown cap on a trunk-like stem gives the mushroom a majestic air. The *Steinpilz* is found in deciduous or coniferous forests or in wooded meadows between the moss and ferns. The *Steinpilz* is suitable for many mushroom dishes and can be dried well.

1 pound fresh yellow boletus (Steinpilz)
or 2 1/2 ounces dried boletus*
1 onion, finely chopped
2 to 3 tablespoons chopped herbs, such as
– thyme
– rosemary
– tarragon
– chervil
– dill
3 to 4 tablespoons oil
1 3/4 cups rice (not parboiled)
1/2 cup red wine
4 cups bouillon
2 tablespoons butter
1 cup Sbrinz or Parmesan, grated

Thoroughly wash and clean mushrooms and chop (soak dried mushrooms 10–15 minutes). Sauté onion, herbs and mushrooms in oil, add rice and sauté. Add wine, reduce by boiling. Gradually add bouillon. Blend butter and cheese with the rice, which should not be overcooked but still moist. Risotto should never be stirred, but, at most, carefully turned with a wooden spoon. It is suitable for all kinds of meat dishes and is also popular in place of a soup when eaten with a salad. It is a matter of personal choice whether red or white wine is served.

* Note: If not available replace with regular mushrooms.

Rice-Leeks

Rispor

The name of this dish is a combination of *Rys* and *Pohr*. It is a risotto with leeks or porrée (from the Latin *Porro*). As we know, borders do not only separate, they can also unite. The construction of the Gotthard Tunnel, in particular, has enabled many influences from Ticino and Italy to make their way into Uri, probably this dish among them.

2 pounds leeks
2 cups bouillon
salt
pepper
nutmeg
1 1/2 cups rice
2 tablespoons butter or shortening
1 cup Bergkäse (mountain cheese), shredded

Slice leeks 1/2″ (1 cm) thick, cook 20 minutes in 2 cups bouillon, season with salt, pepper, nutmeg, add rice and butter, cover and simmer 15 – 20 minutes. If necessary, add water during cooking. Stir rice and leeks, serve hot, garnished with cheese.

Swiss Fried Potatoes

Rösti

Not only do foreigners associate Swiss cuisine with rösti (pronounced *röshti*). Swiss men themselves often evaluate the cooking abilities of their wives solely on the basis of their rösti. Rösti means roasted or fried potatoes. For the peasants, rösti were originally a hearty breakfast. The platter with the grated, golden brown fried potatoes was placed in the middle of the table and everybody began to spoon off from his side. It was customary to dunk the spoon with the potatoes into the café au lait, making the first meal of the day even better.

2 pounds potatoes, boiled in the skins
1 tablespoon salt
3 – 4 tablespoons shortening

Peel and shred potatoes (special rösti shredders are available!) or slice by hand. Sprinkle salt over potatoes. Mix. Heat shortening in skillet. Add potatoes and brown about 30 minutes over low heat while turning occasionally with a spatula. Toward end of frying time compress the potatoes into a solid mass with the spatula and continue to fry until a firm crust has formed. Shake loose or use spatula, turn onto rösti plate. There are, of course, many variations and refinements to this basic recipe, and nearly every canton has its own special rösti. They make a good side-dish for many meals as well as an excellent main course with a salad.

Fried Potatoes à la Bern

Berner Rösti

Rösti from Bern are probably the most famous of these fried potatoes. But nearly every canton has its special way of making them and claims theirs are the best. A short selection:

Basel – with plenty of onion rings;

Ticino – with diced bacon and rosemary;

Zurich – with chopped onion and caraway;

Glarus – with Schabziger cheese;

Appenzell – with elbow macaroni, bacon, Appen-zeller cheese;

Uri – with Bergkäse, onions, coffee;

Western Switzerland – with bacon, tomatoes, paprika, Gruyère.

2 pounds potatoes, boiled in the skins
1 teaspoon salt
2 tablespoons butter
2 tablespoons lard
1/4 cup diced bacon
2 tablespoons milk

Peel potatoes, grate and mix with salt. Heat butter and lard in a skillet. Add bacon and potatoes and brown lightly on all sides, turning occasionally. Compress into a solid mass and cover with lid or roesti plate. Bake 20 minutes over low heat. Then pour milk over potatoes, cover and bake ten minutes more. Turn onto plate and serve.

Perch filets à la Zug

Zuger Rötelfilets

The Rötel is really a lake perch. The variety from Lake Aegeri can be proud of the fact that its ancestors were prized by gourmets as long ago as 1352. At that time, Aegeri was under conscription to the nunnery in Zurich and the monasteries of Kappel and Einsiedeln. The tithe was paid in Rötel, for example, 400 to Kappel annually.

1 1/2 to 2 pounds Rötel filets (or other perch)
salt
pepper
juice of half lemon
butter
1 tablespoon scallions or onion, chopped
1 tablespoon leeks, thinly sliced
1 cup white wine
Sauce:
2 tablespoons butter
salt
pepper
juice of half lemon
1/2 clove of garlic, finely crushed
chives
parsley
marjoram
thyme
1/2 cup cream

Season fish filets with salt, pepper and lemon juice and arrange in a heat-resistant dish. Sprinkle with scallion and leeks, add wine and steam in preheated oven at 350° F (180° C) 10 – 15 minutes (depending on size of filets). Meanwhile, cream butter and mix in the remaining seasonings. Arrange fish filets on serving platter, reduce liquid a little, add herb mixture and cream. Stirring constantly, bring to a boil and pour over fish. Serve with boiled potatoes or rice and green salad. A not-too-heavy white wine goes best.

Swiss Carrot Cake

Rüeblitorte

"Rüebli git schöni Büebli." This proverb from great-grandmother's day means simply that the boys who eat lots of carrots grow up to be especially handsome. In those days, they certainly did not know much about vitamins. Vitamin A, which is very abundant in carrots, was discovered by the English researcher Frederick Gowland Hopkins early in this century. Important work on the topic of vitamins was done in the Bunge School in Basel, where pioneering experiments were done on mice in 1881. Another famous Swiss, the physician Dr. Maximilian Bircher-Benner, pointed out, the importance of vitamin A when he said, "It is impossible to underestimate the importance of natural foods including foods rich in Vitamin A in the daily diet."

6 eggs
1 1/2 cups sugar
grated peel of one lemon
1 shot glass kirschwasser (cherry brandy)
3 cups grated almonds (11 ounces)
1/2 pound grated raw carrots
3 tablespoons flour
powdered sugar
12 carrots made of marzipan (for decoration)

Separate egg yolks from egg white. Beat egg-yolks with sugar until fluffly. Add lemon peel and kirschwasser. Alternately fold stiffly whipped egg whites with the almonds, carrots and flour into the egg-yolk mixture. Turn into a greased and floured springform. Bake at medium heat 350° F (180° C) about one hour, until lightly browned. Dust with powdered sugar. Garnish with carrots made of marzipan. The carrot cake tastes best after one to two days!

Sauerkraut
à la Schaffhausen

Sauerkraut nach Schaffhauser Art

It is known that Galenus, a famous physician who lived around 200 B.C., recommended sauerkraut for stomach disorders, gout and bites from rabid dogs. Even today, the characteristics of fermented cabbage are praised, for example, its easy digestibility, high vitamin content and good taste. No wonder it is so popular all over central Europe and is prepared in so many ways. Under the Munot, the symbol of Schaffhausen, people like sauerkraut with the special caraway sausages of this town on the Rhine Falls, with a touch of Marc, spirits made from the pressed grapes of the local vineyards.

3 large onions
2 tablespoons shortening
2 pounds sauerkraut
1 tablespoon caraway seeds
1 tablespoon juniper berries
1 cup bouillon
1 shot glass Marc de Schaffhouse*
2 tablespoons cornstarch
4 caraway sausages (or other country pork sausage)

Sauté chopped onions in oil. Loosely heap sauerkraut on top, sprinkle with caraway and juniper berries and add bouillon. Simmer loosely covered until soft, stirring occasionally. Mix the Marc with cornstarch, add to sauerkraut and briefly bring to a boil. Warm the caraway sausages 10 minutes in the hot sauerkraut. Serve with boiled potatoes or leavened dark bread. Serve hard cider or a cold beer to drink.

* Marc de Schaffhouse is a clear brandy like many other fruit spirits such as Schnaps, Grappa, Aquavit, Slivovič etc. and can be substituted by these.

Schabziger Potatoes

Schabziger-Kartoffeln

Schabziger is without doubt one of the oldest cheeses in Switzerland. It was first mentioned around 1000 B.C. The Glarner issued exact regulations on the production of the cheese in 1464 and created a trade mark. *Ziger*, often spelled *Zieger*, is made by additional acidification and heating of the watery part of the milk (whey), which separates during cheese-making. The piquant Glarner herb cheese is augmented with herbs and spices, one of the most important of which is the Ziger Clover, the *Zigerchruut* (trigonella coerulea.) This herb has a pungent smell and was brought to Europe from Asia Minor in the late 11th century by the Crusaders. The Glarner were introduced to it in the Saeckingen monastery, where it was grown along with many other kitchen herbs. They subsequently grew it themselves and used it to give their *Ziger* its very characteristic aroma.

3/4 pounds potatoes
salt water
3 cups elbow macaroni
1/3 to 1/2 cup Schabziger cheese, shredded
3 tablespoons butter in small pieces
1 1/2 tablespoons butter
2 tablespoons fine bread crumbs

Peel potatoes, cook in salt water until soft. Also cook noodles in salt water al dente, i.e., not too soft; drain well. Arrange potatoes and noodles alternately with layers of shredded Schabziger in between in a bowl. Heat butter and briefly brown bread crumbs in it. Pour over potatoes and noodles and serve hot. Salad in season and a glass of light red wine go well with this dish.

Leg of Mutton à la Chur

Churer Schafstotzen

"Potatoes, as the farmers say, taste good on any day!" In the many Swiss country casseroles, potatoes are often the main ingredient. They blend, however, so well with fats, meats and vegetables that nobody ever seems to get tired of them. An old saying has it that potatoes are filling but not fattening. Along these lines, we would like to point out a fact which not everyone knows, that 1/2 lb. of boiled potatoes contain only 155 calories, not very many!

1 leg of mutton
salt
pepper
1 clove garlic
3 tablespoons shortening
4 carrots, halved, lengthwise
whole cloves
1 onion
1 1/2 cups bouillon
2 1/4 pound potatoes

Salt and pepper leg of mutton and lace with garlic slivers. Heat fat in a copper roasting pan add meat, peeled carrots and an onion studded with whole cloves. Pour 3/4 cups of bouillon over everything and roast at 400° F (200° C), turning and hasting often, for 1 3/4 hours. About 3/4 of an hour before end of roasting period, add peeled potatoes cut in large pieces to roasting pan and stretch gravy with bouillon. An excellent beer is brewed in Chur. But the wine is also good there. How about a Churer Schiller? (Rosé wine)

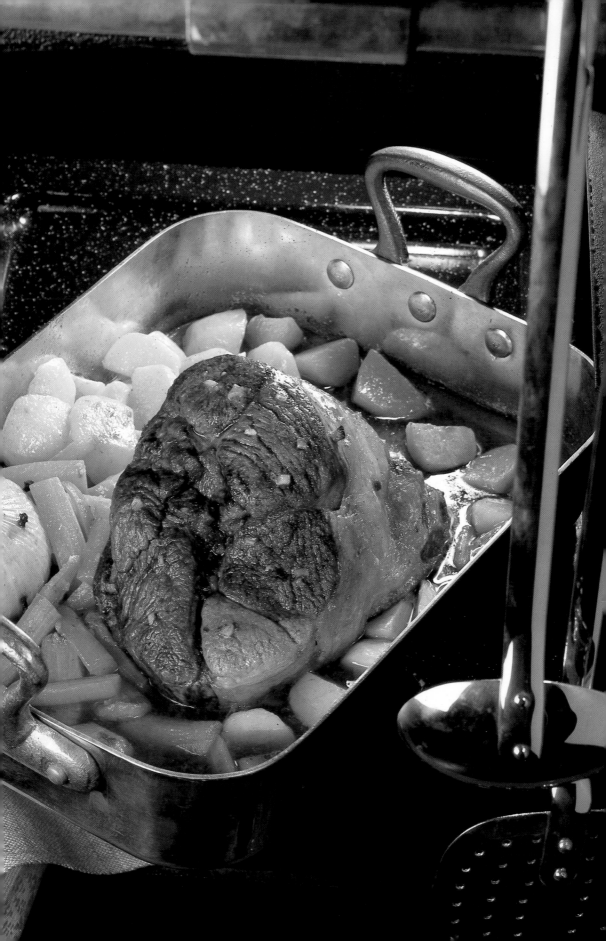

Emmentaler Mutton Stew

Emmentaler Schafsvoressen

We can no longer be sure where the strange word
Voressen (lit. hors d'œuvre) comes from, for the
things that carry this name today are usually quite
hearty and nourishing. But it probably did mean an
appetizer, *Vorspeise,* at one time, and when today
we think of *Voressen* as a type of ragout, then this
French name hints at an appetizer, to tickle your
palate, and the world-famous *Ragout-fin* is indeed
one of the classical appetizers.
In the Emmental, the Schafsvoressen is very popular and the Sichlete, the thanksgiving feast, is
unthinkable without it. This recipe comes from
Langnau in the Emmental.

3 pounds mutton, cubed
3 1/3 cups mutton or beef bouillon
1 bay leaf
1 onion studded with whole cloves
1 carrot
5 tablespoons flour
3/4 cup hard cider or white wine
salt
pepper
nutmeg
cream
butter
saffron

Heat the bouillon with the bay leaf, the onion and
the carrot, add meat and boil until meat is done.
Bind the liquid with the flour blended with cider or
wine, season with salt, pepper and nutmeg. Refine
sauce with cream, butter and saffron according to
taste. The sauce can also be finished with cream
and egg-yolk. Serve with mashed potatoes.

Deep-Fried Swiss Pastries

Schenkeli

This pre-Lenten pastry is deep-fried. How do you determine the correct temperature of the fat? Our grandmothers put the handle of a wooden spoon in the fat. As soon as little bubbles formed around the wood, the fat was the right temperature. The old-fashioned Swiss cuisine has numerous *Chüchli*, most of them deep-fried in lard, which are served at Carnival time, parish fairs, or on long winter evenings at get-togethers with the spinning wheels. There was, and is, cider or wine and lots of fun!

11 ounces shortening
2 1/2 cups sugar
10 eggs
grated peel of one lemon
3 1/4 pounds flour (11 1/4 cups)
1 teaspoon baking powder
shortening for deep frying

Cream shortening, sugar and eggs until light. Add lemon peel, flour and baking powder and knead into a dough. Roll out finger-sized *Schenkeli*, about 2″ to 3″ (5 – 7 cm) long. Crease the top of each *Schenkeli* with index finger. Heat sufficient shortening in a large pan to 340° F (170° C.) Fry several *Schenkeli* at one time, remove with a screen dipper (*see* picture page 196 upper right), drain and place on paper towels. These ingredients make almost 100 *Schenkeli*. You can halve the ingredients or fry a certain supply to keep the pantry stocked.

Apples on Top

Schnitz und drunder

"In my days," old people sometimes tell us, "mother still had her bin of dried fruit in the attic." These dried fruit bins were never empty, for every fall a new supply of dried fruit was prepared. It was marvelous for the children to visit Grandmother in the winter. She would stick her hand into the fruit bin every now and then and distribute pieces of dried apples or pears. This recipe for "dried apples on top" is still popular, and this time we have potatoes underneath.

1/2 pound dried, sweet apple slices
3/4 pound thick-sliced bacon
1 1/4 pound potatoes
salt
butter

In a pan, barely cover the apple slices with lukewarm water and soak overnight. Cook in soaking water with bacon, covered, about one hour over medium heat. Peel and slice potatoes, place on the cooked apples and bacon, lightly sprinkle with salt and cook until potatoes are done. Remove bacon from pan, add flakes of butter to potatoes and apples in the pot, allow to melt. Lightly shake potatoes and apple slices to mix (do not stir), place bacon slices on top and serve.

Barley Soup

Schoppa da jotta

Barley (hordeum distichum) is the one grain which, in contrast to the others, grows in nearly every climate on earth. It grows in the tropics and in the Himalayas. There it can be found at an altitude of 13,000 feet (4,300 metres), in the Andes up to 9,000 feet (3,000 metres) and in the Alps up to 6,000 feet (2,100 metres). Characteristics of barley are its resistance, its short vegetation period and its low moisture requirements. That is why it is grown primarily in mountainous areas and northerly regions. Barley is highly nutritious, which was particularly important, of course, in the meals of the mountain farmers. This barley soup comes from the Engadine and is popular throughout the canton Graubünden. It is perhaps the most famous dish in the region. It is made with variations in almost every household.

1 1/4 pounds smoked beef (20 ounces)
1 cup barley
1 small head of cabbage
1/2 pound potatoes, peeled and cut in strips
1 tablespoon flour
3 tablespoons cream
salt
pepper

Add meat and barley to 7 cups water and after two hours of boiling add the chopped vegetables and potatoes. Simmer one more hour, then blend flour with cream and add to soup, season with salt and pepper and prepare for serving by cutting meat into cubes. Engadine sausages can also be added to this thick soup.

Pork Stew

Schtunggis

In Swiss-German dialect, *Schtunggis* means something like thick mush. One schtunggt (mashes) something to sauce (apples) or mush (mashed potatoes). There is often a *Gschtungg* (a pushing crowd) at the movies or theatre. Nor is it very pleasant to be inegschtungget (pushed in) from behind into a streetcar! This dish itself is famous all over central Switzerland, especially in the cantons Obwalden and Nidwalden. As with almost all native Swiss dishes, it is of peasant origin. It probably got its name in earlier days when the peasant families would set a pot with all ingredients on the stove or in the oven and then went out to work the fields. This did not allow for precise cooking times and when, occasionally, everyone returned later than had been expected, the potatoes had fallen apart and the dish was mush, a *Schtunggis*.

1 1/4 pounds lean pork, cubed
1 – 2 tablespoons shortening
2 onions
salt
pepper
nutmeg
2 pounds vegetables such as leeks, carrots,
kohlrabi, celery, (vary according to season)
2 cups bouillon
4 – 5 potatoes

Brown meat in hot fat. Add chopped onions and brown. Season with salt, pepper and nutmeg. Cut vegetables into small pieces and layer alternately with meat in a pot with a tightfitting cover. Add half the bouillon and braise one hour in pre-heated oven. Add the peeled and cubed potatoes and the remaining bouillon and braise 30 minutes longer.

Valais Wedding Dessert

Sii

This dessert used to be served at wedding dinners in Valais. Our recipe represents a modified, modern version, since the rye bread and the elderberry syrup of Valais is not available everywhere. The poet Ludwig Imesch had this to say about the wines from Valais, "The waters of glaciers – channelled through wooden troughs over steep cliffs – give the grapes the strenght to produce noble juice – the wine – born of water – for the pleasure and the sorrow of man, whether he enjoys it in pleasant moderation or wastes it in excess."

6 slices white bread, toasted
1 bottle Valais red wine (Dôle)*
5 tablespoons sugar
2/3 cup raisins
3 tablespoons butter
1 tablespoon red currant jelly

Toast bread lightly on both sides and place in a baking dish. Pour wine over bread and sprinkle with sugar. Add raisins, butter and jelly and simmer 10 minutes in the oven or on the stove. The original recipe is made with 1/2 lb Valais rye bread which is cut into small cubes and soaked overnight in 2 cups Dôle. Soak the raisins in the remaining wine overnight. Combine and add sugar, and instead of currant jelly, use elderberry syrup (see recipe page 104). Melt butter in a caquelon (fondue dish or chafing dish) and warm the mixture, but not too much so that the wine does not evaporate. Fill into pretty dessert dishes and serve with whipped cream.

* Note: If Dôle is not available other light red wines (Burgundy type) will do fine.

Cheese Soufflé

Soufflé au fromage

Translated literally, a soufflé is something blown up, and, in fact, the heat of the oven does blow up this dish. The compositions of soufflés is lighter than that of other casseroles and therefore soufflés must be treated with more care. The stiffly whipped egg whites play the main rôle, the expanding agent. Salty soufflés are usually served as appetizers or as easily digestible main dishes. Sweet soufflés, on the other hand, are intended as desserts.

1 1/4 cups milk
5 egg yolks
1 cup Sbrinz or Parmesan, grated
salt
pepper
1 pinch nutmeg
1 tablespoon cornstarch
5 egg whites
2 tablespoons butter
bread crumbs

In a large bowl, mix milk, egg yolks, cheese, seasonings and cornstarch well. Then whip egg whites until very stiff and carefully fold them into the cheese mixture. Butter a soufflé dish well, all the way to the top, coat with bread crumbs and fill with soufflé mixture two-thirds full. Distribute remaining butter in small pieces on top. Bake at medium heat in preheated oven 20 – 30 minutes, until it has risen nicely and is browned on top. Do not open oven door during baking – the soufflé will collapse! Remove from oven shortly before serving. Serve with green salad and a red wine from Lake Geneva.

Spinach Noodles à la Glarus

Glarner Spinatzoggle

Hieronymus Bock, author of one of the most famous books on herbs, wrote in 1550 about the spinach native to Switzerland, "Of all the cooking herbs, the spinach herb is, in my opinion, the best and loveliest!" He also had something to say about the "inner and outer *effects*" of spinach. "Spinach softens the belly, soothes the raw throat, and improves the breath. Said medicine is also good for the stomach and liver, for it kills the pain!" Spinach has its name from the Latin *Spinacia*, and the Swiss dialect has made *Schbinätsch* or *Binätsch* out of that. Zoggle, by the way, are related to the Swabian knöpfli and spätzle.

2 1/2 cups flour
3/4 cups water
1 1/2 teaspoons salt
3 eggs
3/4 pounds leaf spinach
1 bunch parsley
3 – 4 tablespoons grated Schabziger cheese
2 – 3 tablespoons butter

Make a smooth dough from flour, water, salt and beaten eggs. Briefly blanch spinach, drain well and chop finely. Mix dough and spinach well; add finely chopped parsley. Bring lightly salted water to a boil in a large pot and pass the dough in portions through a knöpfli strainer (see picture, upper left) or press through a Spätzle colander into the water. Simmer. As soon as the Zoggles rise to the surface, remove them with a screen dipper (see picture, upper right), drain and arrange on a pre-heated platter. Sprinkle each layer with finely grated Schabziger. Melt butter and sprinkle over the Zoggles. Serve with fresh salad.

Herb Dip

Stupfete

In this case "stupfen" means "to dip in". This dish from Eastern Switzerland is an amusing change for a nice evening's entertainment because, as in the case of fondue, everybody sits around the table and uses the saucepan in the center. By the way, potatoes have many different names, and as late as one hundred years ago the selection of varieties was so great it was confusing. There were some which were named after the time they matured, for example, the *Drümonet Härdöpfel* (the earliest, which matures in three months), or the *Jaköbler,* a potato which was ready to harvest around St. Jakob's Day, July 25. *Augschte Härdöpfel* was also known, and it isn't hard to guess that this one was ready to be harvested in August. For our recipe, small new potatoes are best.

2 1/4 pounds potatoes
8 tablespoons oil
4 onions, finely chopped
2 bunches parsley, finely chopped
2 bunches chives, finely cut
pepper
salt
8 tablespoons vinegar or white wine

Boil potatoes in their skins until soft. Heat oil in a small pan or fondue caquelon, then add onions, parsley, chives, pepper and salt, vinegar or white wine, stir, and simmer about 5 minutes. The dip should be brought to the table boiling hot and set in the middle of the table on an alcohol burner for community use. Each diner "stupft", dunks a piece of potato at the tip of a fork into the dip before eating it. A cool Thurgau wine, such as one from Lake Constance, goes well with this. Any good white wine will do as well.

Pork Rump with Sour Potatoes

Süübäggli und suure Gummeli

(5 – 6 servings)

Well, now we've really gotten into Schwyzer-dütsch, the "original" Swiss-German dialect! Let us, therefore, "translate" a few of the dialect expressions for our non-Swiss guests:

Süü – Säue, Schweine (Schwyz) = sow, pigs
Souw – Sau, Schwein (Lucerne) = sow, swine
Söi, Seu – Säue (Lucerne) = plural
Schwynigs – Schweinefleisch = pork
Bäggli – Backen, Wangen = cheek
Gummeli – Kartoffeln (Schwyz) = potatoes

3 to 4 1/2 pounds fresh (not smoked) ham
8 bay leaves
8 whole cloves
2 1/2 pounds potatoes
4 tablespoons flour
4 tablespoons butter
4 cups bouillon
1 bay leaf
1 whole clove
1 pinch nutmeg
3 tablespoons vinegar
1/2 cup cream
1 bunch parsley

Place pork in hot but not boiling water and let steep (do not boil) 2 to 2 1/4 hours (depending on weight). Remove and remove heavy layer of skin. Slash remaining layer of fat crosswise. Pin the bay leaves and cloves around the ham and brown it about 30 minutes in the oven. Peel potatoes and slice 1/4″ (1/2 cm) thick. Brown flour in butter, add bouillon and stir until smooth. Add bay leaf, clove and potato slices. Cook over low heat until done. Carefully season with nutmeg. Mix vinegar and cream and add. Remove bay leaf and clove and serve the potatoes with the meat. Garnish with chopped parsley.

Tomatoes à la Valais

Walliser Tomatenspeise

Originally, the tomato grew as a wild tropical plant in the Peruvian Andes. The Indians were growing them as food when the Spaniards got there. In 1498 Christopher Columbus brought a few tomato plants to Europe. At first it was considered to be only a rare decorative plant. They were first commercially raised in Switzerland in 1915. Many variations in color and shape soon appeared. Tomatoes from the size of a currant to that of two fists, from white to all shades of yellow and from brick red to wine red. Today the tomato has become one of the most important vegetables on the European market. The fruit contains many minerals and vitamins necessary to good health.

4 large tomatoes
some butter
2 to 3 cloves of garlic
or 1 onion, finely chopped
herbs
pepper
oregano
paprika
8 small eggs

Halve tomatoes horizontally, remove some of the pulp, place tomato pulp in a greased baking dish. Sprinkle with garlic or onion, season. Season the hollowed-out tomato halves on the inside and place in the dish, open side down. Bake about 15 minutes in a hot oven. Remove and break an egg into each half, season again, and bake another 6–8 minutes – with the open side up – in the oven. Serve tomatoes with the sauce and with either rice or noodles. The wine: a light Dôle (red wine).

Tomatoes à la Fribourg

Tomates fribourgeoises

The French, full of great expectations, call the tomato the love apple, while the more sober English
and German speaking people used the derivation
from the historical name *tumatle americanorum*,
which has been assumed by nearly all languages.
Red is, of course, the color of love, and people
used to think that eating such a bright red fruit could
arouse passion. The Society for Swiss Folklore re-
ports that in Western Switzerland around 1762 the
tomato was considered an infallible aphrodesiac.
The Austrians call them paradise apples, the Italians
say *pomodoro*, golden apple. And, indeed, tomatoes really were more golden yellow than bright
red at one time. It was not until the mid-18th century when Italian growers were sucessful in achiev-
ing the bright red color.

1 pound tomatoes
salt
1 cup Gruyère cheese, finely diced or shredded
1/2 cup potatoes, finely diced, boiled
1 onion, chopped
1 tablespoon chives, finely cut
pepper

Halve tomatoes, hollow out a little, salt and let stand
a while. Then discard the resulting liquid and fill
the tomatoes with a mixture of finely diced cheese,
diced potatoes, chopped onion and pepper. Bake
the tomatoes 10–15 minutes and garnish with
chives. Serve with French bread and Pinot Noir
wine.

Fried Corn-Meal Lumps

Türken-Ribel

Ribel is an ancient dish, known primarily in the Ratian Alps (Graubünden and the southern regions of the canton St. Gallen). The Turkish adjective hints at corn, which is also called Turkish grain in dialect since this grain was probably introduced into Europe in the 16th century from the Osman Empire. In Romansh the dish is called *maluns*. The *Ribel* is usually eaten like fondue, from a community platter or pan. It was customary to dip a spoonful of *Ribel* in the café au lait on the way to the mouth!

2 cups corn meal, fine grind
3/4 cups wheat flour
3/4 to 1 cup water
5 tablespoons butter
2 tablespoons butter

Blend corn meal and flour well in a bowl and gradually add the lightly salted, boiling water to the bowl while constantly stirring. Continue stirring until lumps (the *Ribeli*) form. Let stand one hour. Heat butter in a skillet and toast the *Ribeli* until they are brown. Add fresh butter to the *Türggeribel* and serve with café au lait or salad.

Plum Casserole

Zwetschgenauflauf

Small rolls of milk, butter or egg dough, *Weggli,* have been baked in Switzerland since times immemorial. They used to be called *Chrüzerbrötli* or *Batzebrötli* because they cost a *Kreuzer* or a *Batzen.* Reason enough to serve them only on special occasions. The white rolls were, of course, very treasured as a change from the usual dark bread. From this period we probably also get the expression, "That goes like hot Weggli" (equivalent to, "That's going like hotcakes!"). Canton Basel is known for its sweet tooth, and the Basler goodies have been discussed on another page of this book.

4 rolls
2 cups milk
3 tablespoons raisins
2 1/2 pounds Italian plums
2 eggs
5 tablespoons sugar
2 tablespoons butter
1/2 teaspoon cinnamon
1/2 teaspoon grated lemon peel
2 tablespoons grated almonds or hazelnuts

Cut rolls into 1/2" (1 cm) cubes, pour hot milk over them, cover and let stand 10 minutes, until bread is soft and all liquid soaked up. Soak raisins in a little water. Halve plums and remove pits. Beat egg-yolks and sugar, add soft butter. Add cinnamon, lemon peel, drained raisins, almonds or hazelnuts, plums and rolls. Immediately before baking fold in the stiffly whipped egg whites. Turn mixture into a well buttered casserole, top with pieces of butter and bake 35 minutes at 430°F (220°C).

References of Photographs

Comet 30
Siegfried Eigstler 32/33
Edmond van Hoorick 2, 6/7 (8), 14/15 (5), 16/17,
    18l., 26/27, 35, 36/37 (6), 42/43 (3), 44/45 (4),
    47, 48/49 (5), 50, 51, 52, 54/55 (7), 58/59
Löbl-Schreyer 29
Sirius Bildarchiv/Döbbelin 60–209
Verlagsarchiv 11
Richard Weich 22/23 (8), 38/39
ZEFA-Linthom 19

Recipes Classified by Groups

**Unless otherwise indicated,
all recipes are for four servings.**

Recipes in Alphabetical Order

In our cookbook series

Kulinarische Streifzüge

the following volumes
have already been
published in German

Schwaben **Baden**

Bayern **Franken**

Hessen **Pfalz**

Rheinland **Westfalen**

Friesland **Niedersachsen**

Deutschland **Österreich**

Schweiz **Jugoslawien**

Toskana **Ungarn**

also available in English:

Culinary Excursions through Germany

SIGLOCH
EDITION